How Artists Make Money

&

How Money Makes Artists

by

David Berry

Coach House Books, Toronto

first edition

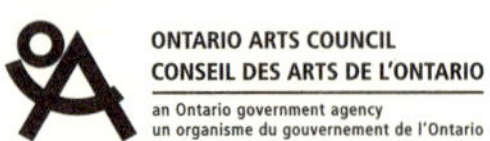

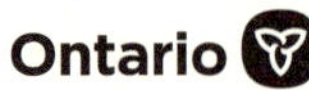

Published with the generous assistance of the Canada Council for the Arts and the Ontario Arts Council. Coach House Books also acknowledges the support of the Government of Canada through the Canada Book Fund and the Government of Ontario through the Ontario Book Publishing Tax Credit.

LIBRARY AND ARCHIVES CANADA CATALOGUING IN PUBLICATION

Title: How artists make money & how money makes artists / by David Berry.
Other titles: How artists make money and how money makes artists
Names: Berry, David, author
Identifiers: Canadiana (print) 20250225484 | Canadiana (ebook) 20250227932 | ISBN 9781552455067 (softcover) | ISBN 9781770568648 (EPUB) | ISBN 9781770568655 (PDF)
Subjects: LCSH: Arts—Economic aspects. | LCSH: Arts and society. | LCSH: Artists—Economic conditions. | LCSH: Artists—Employment. | LCSH: Cultural industries—Economic aspects.
Classification: LCC NX634 .B47 2025 | DDC 338.4/77—dc23

How Money Makes Artists and How Artists Make Money is available as an ebook: ISBN 978 1 77056 864 8 (EPUB), ISBN 978 1 77056 865 5 (PDF)

Purchase of the print version of this book entitles you to a free digital copy. To claim your ebook of this title, please email sales@chbooks.com with proof of purchase. (Coach House Books reserves the right to terminate the free digital download offer at any time.)

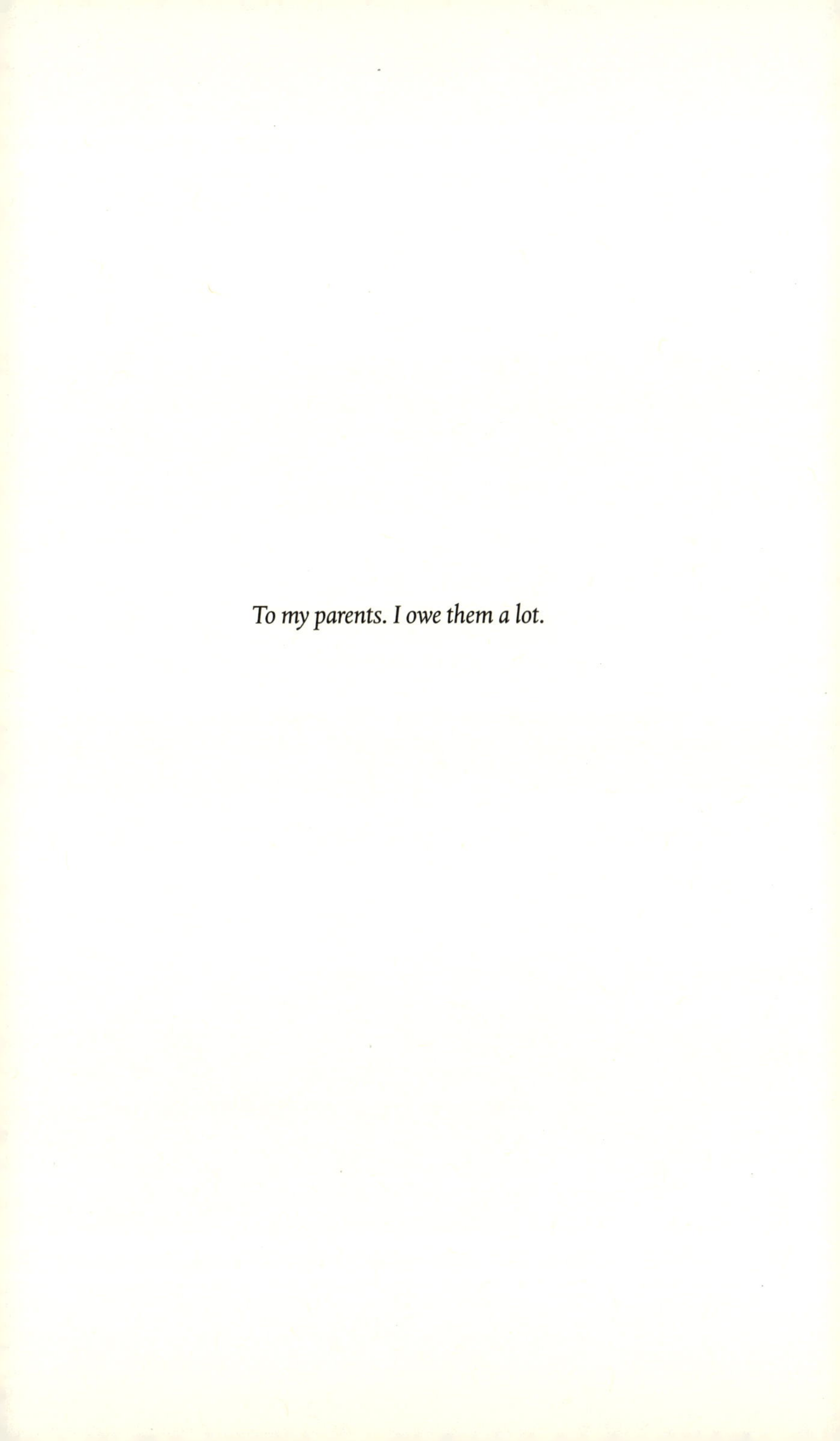

To my parents. I owe them a lot.

Table of Contents

Introduction:
Somebody Has to Bring in a Little Money

*When I was ten years old, I was rich, I was an aristocrat. Riding around
in taxis, surrounded by comfort, and all I thought about was art and
music. Now, I'm thirty-six, and all I think about is money.*
> — Wally, *My Dinner With André*

Here, with the pithy disdain for money only an aristocrat
can afford to have, Wallace Shawn sums up the late-
twentieth-century belief that art and money are, if not directly
opposed, best left apart. This is still a thing in the early twenty-
first century, but it seems to have become less widespread
now that money has thoroughly trumped every other consideration for what constitutes a good life – from creative expression to, you know, the continued existence of civilization.
Zeitgeist or not, it's not exactly wrong.

Probably the strongest argument for art as the highest
aspiration of humanity is that you need to use art to argue
about it. Math pulls the same trick, but eventually you need
to explain to someone what math is, and that's where art
comes in. In practical terms, art is why we know *we* are we.

At both its most basic and profound levels, we use art to
show we understand each other. Art is a document of its
creator's entire understanding of the world; we bring our
entire understanding of the world to try to interpret it. Often,
we respond to how much it matches our own experience
and captures our own internal states. Art is communication,
turning abstract expressions into concrete meanings, and
conveying feelings across common understandings. It both

relies on and creates the context of the world around it. Art of any kind endures because it captures some understanding, some piece of the world, so purely that it becomes a piece of the world itself. Time spent thinking about art is time spent wondering what it really feels like to be you. It's not the only reason we're here, but it's a question we should answer.

———————

On the flip side, money is a pretty good way to count stuff. That is not to say counting stuff isn't really important to the advancement of our species, or even our individual selves. You could make an excellent case that money has done as much as anything to help us search for those answers: it has bought us the time to do so, after introducing us to the idea that time needs to be bought in the first place. Now, thousands of years into money – it came well after the artistic impulse but not so long after cities – it's easy to see the downside, but you can also see why we adopted money in the first place. The first way it gave us more time, if the introductory economics textbooks are to be believed, was by saving us from having to make multiple intermediary trades to turn our goats into bread. You give me money, I give someone else the money, we all get what we want – it really simplified things.

One reason art and money feel so opposed is that art tends to complicate things while money simplifies them. Just like art, money turns abstract understandings into concrete realities: it turns the concept of a goat, or the time spent baking bread, into coins and bills and credit statements. The goal of money is always to make things more efficient: it's communication without need for any further context. Which frees us up from some mental effort, but then binds us in a world where money is the only meaningful context. Money defines our every aspect, limits us to how we get it and what we can do with it. Art makes us more human and money makes us less, but with the promise that we can *do* so much more. Art might be more fundamental, but the reason we are no longer doing it on clay tablets and cave walls is because of the world money has created. Money didn't create art, but a lot less art would have been possible if we hadn't come up with money. Part of the discomfort of putting art next to money is the recognition that money is the more powerful force.

But if you want to make the case that money has made us overall better humans, or conversely make the case that it has diminished our fundamental humanity entirely, you need to use ideas and techniques shaped by art, if not art itself. Art is how we understand the world; money is how we have the time to understand the world. But the goal of money isn't to help us understand the world, it's to create more opportunities for money. It gives us time, but then overwhelms it, dictates it, crowds out the possibility of our using it for experiencing or creating. Money is often treated like a polluting force in art, but it's more of an extinction-level threat. No one makes anything they can't afford to. Money doesn't have to destroy things; it can prevent them entirely. One of the things money seems to prevent is our ability to talk about it, whether that's because of sheer power or plain fear. Embedded in Wally's complaint is the cultural belief that it's not polite to talk about money; it's crass and rude to even think about it.

So let's talk about money.

———

However we want to define it, art would exist without money. In this book, I've been exceedingly broad in my definition of art – poetry, theatre, painting, prose, dance, music (both performance and recording), film, television, and YouTube all factor in. All of them have at times, sometimes concurrently, been both art and not art. But there's never been anywhere that people didn't paint and dance and tell each other stories.

Artists absolutely wouldn't exist without money, though. By the rules of money, it's just like any other job: it's defined, refined, and determined by who's paying. As you might have guessed from what I consider art, I'm tempted to be liberal with the term 'artist.' But even then I would have to define it against the basic logic of money: you are an artist if you get paid to make art. Anyone at all can make art, but you only get to call yourself an artist if you're paid for it. That reads like a tautology to an economic mind but feels disgustingly restrictive to the creative one. The creative mind, however, doesn't matter here: people are paying for art because it gives them status, confirms their position in society, affirms their impeccable taste. They are not honouring the artist's talents or spirit or creative spark – though some of the first people to start paying artists well insisted that the importance of honouring such qualities was the reason art was worth what they were paying.

Art began as a way to honour the gods, or whatever animating spirit we once believed in, and artists almost universally began as *instruments* to honour the gods. Richer people began paying them as a way to prove their pious devotion to gods, which incidentally was quite a good way to justify all the money they had. Both of those justifications survived for a very long time. Gradually, practising art became a way to signify an enlightened soul, and paying artists became a way to signify an enlightened soul who couldn't make art but did have money. The term 'artist' was created by people of immense wealth, power, and position to justify that wealth, power, and position, and it was accepted by artists to justify their fees or, where those weren't high enough, prestige and position.

That basic dynamic has remained the same, even as power, wealth, and position have gotten a little more diffused. Now governments pay artists to prove the strength of their national or cultural character, to justify their existence as recognizable states with traditions and meanings of their very own. Art has been turned over to the market, and some artists now create industrial-level products that support vast interconnected webs of jobs. Entire art industries are buoyed by the still-intact prestige of the artist, even as those same industries use that prestige as leverage to spread the money an artist generates further and further away from the artist. The term 'artist' has lived up to its restrictive simplicity, often excluding entire ways of creating and huge numbers of creators because no one found it useful to justify paying them. The financial understanding of the term has so clouded our view that we have trouble understanding something as art unless it's been made by an officially recognized artist. Once you were an artist because you were paid to make art; now you're not regarded as making art unless you're being paid for it. Money has come to define the whole thing. One of the easiest ways to tell what new kinds of art are emerging – to figure out who will be elevated into the realm of artist – is to figure out which kinds of creative acts people are getting paid more for; 'follow the money' works as well for artists as for any other aspect of contemporary life.

Artists have always followed from money: its locus of power, prestige, and influence grants them whatever legitimacy they have. Money created the concept of artists, sustains their ideal, and allows them to cling to this vaunted self-definition for as long as they are useful to the people who control the money. It might be fun for us to debate what really is an art form and which practitioners really are artists, but the answer bludgeons us with cold simplicity: art is what the people who pay for art say it is, and artists are the people they pay for it. Anything else is an argument in search of a patron.

———

The order of the words in this book's title is not happenstance. I began with the goal of figuring out how and why artists get money. My bias was that people will create no matter their circumstances, but it's important to understand the circumstances that lead to people creating. In trying to untangle that thread, I realized just how instrumental payment is to how we even understand artists – in the here and now, and through history. I'm not enthused by this realization, but – whether through an arty devotion to the truth that I perceive, or my inability to escape the system I was born in – it's where I am now. I hope it's clear my sympathies remain with everyone who makes art. I hope I can convince people to make it easier to make art, whatever that ends up costing. You can put a price on anything, but the price doesn't have to be what matters.

Obviously this is a personal subject. I have in the course of writing this particular book been forced to confront whether I even am an artist. I certainly consider myself one, if not much of a financially successful one, but financial questions have come to dominate how I think about what I do. I started off as a journalist and critic, helping to popularize and interpret art, until that field narrowed sharply. I figured that if I was not going to make much of a living at it, I might as well have the freedom to follow my nose. I wrote a book and quickly realized that even my relative advantages couldn't make up for how little money there is in art that doesn't fit inside narrow and prescribed lanes. I have a supportive family – psychologically and materially – and the ability to make a stable living whenever I choose. Both of these are essential to making any go of it, but they are also arguments against pouring excessive time and resources into something that is, in monetary terms, a public hobby. And if I, as materially comfortable a specimen as Canadian public schools have produced in the last forty years, can't make a go of it despite having the requisite skills and abilities, what sort of shot do the vast swath of people have who are in my position or worse? No wonder they have my sympathies.

Writing this book may have convinced me of the crushing power money has over art and artists, but it has also under-lined my love for their perseverance. Artists, from the perspective of the people who keep them around, are effec-tively just jewels with a spiritual compass – handmaidens of power, jesters, the pretty little thing kept around because it makes one feel good, etc. Yet artists have never lost their power to create transcendent things. Every society's art that we can still access vibrates intensely through the human experience. We are still creating things that can fundamentally alter people's lives, shake the core of their understanding, rewrite their entire personhood. The drive to create still stands outside of money: people will squeeze it into the cracks of their lives, sacrifice comfort or even necessity, fight and claw and carve out time to make something, to share their understanding of the world. They shouldn't have to, but goddammit, they do.

To me, the biggest danger of continuing to let money define art and artists is that it can strangle that individual drive to create. We, the collective, will keep making things, but there is real tragedy in the number of individuals who will never get the chance because they have no way to make it pay. By being upfront about the power that money has over art, we can, I hope, drain some of that power – at least to the point that you, the person reading this, believe in the power of art enough to keep paying for it.

I am joking. I think. I do hope you leave here with the belief that thinking about art is a nobler, more exciting pursuit than thinking about money. I also hope you'll understand that most artists never make the kind of money commensurate with following your noblest, most exciting ideals. But if the point of art is to know ourselves, and the point of an artist is to make art, we'd better know what money has done to us.

So let's talk about artists and money.

1: Next to Godliness
From One Creative Force to Another

Maybe it's a little romantic or naive, but I think part of the point of sharing art is to give people something that cannot properly be valued. When I think about the works of art that have shook and shaped my life – El Greco's electric canvases, Vonnegut's sardonic humanism, Wu-Tang's nerdy aggressiveness, Altman's swirling slice-of-life films – I can't put any price on that. When you create, you sign up for an unequal relationship.

The problems start when the unequal part of the relationship becomes the entirety of the relationship. In his rather droll book *Why Are Artists Poor? The Exceptional Economy of the Arts*, Dutch economist and visual artist Hans Abbing tries to explain why artists are almost universally acknowledged to never get what they're really worth. This is true most obviously of your classic starving artist, but it applies even to your rich, household-name artists, who see only a fraction of the overall economic activity their work generates. (According to Abbing, the fact that these people are rich artists more often comes down to their business acumen more than their abilities as artists, which certainly doesn't change the basic math.) As artists will be the first to tell you, artists do not get a fair deal.

Abbing attributes this to a gift mentality. As he describes it, an essential part of the value of art – in spiritual or psychological or other airy, artistic, ineffable, non-monetary terms – is precisely that it embraces its status as beyond mere commerce, mere money. It's tempting to think of art as outside of our practical needs: art does not hold up walls or keep us warm; it derives its value from our perceptions of it. It exists to prove we are capable of appreciating things beyond their practicality. We can see again how it is directly opposed to the inherent efficiency of money: if art were so crass as to be a mere functionary of the market logic that otherwise dominates our world, it would lose its stature, from which it derives its monetary worth.

The point of money is to help you acquire things you don't have. In the case of the artist, what patrons are buying is less the produced work than proof of some spiritual capacity they might otherwise seem to lack. If you frame the purchase as rewarding the artist for their extraordinary talents and sensitivities, what you are really buying is proof that you are capable of recognizing such talents and sensitivities – you elevate yourself by elevating the artist. The artist necessarily becomes more than just a seller of wares, they become someone worthy of recognition – the money is not payment, it is tribute. This contradiction not only makes it exceedingly hard for the artist to get a fair deal, it actively discourages a fair deal. Creating things for a living is not supposed to be a mere job; it is an imperative of the soul, a calling, a purpose. Doing it just to make your crust makes you a bad artist, deficient of the higher concerns necessary to make really good art. Artists are poor, at least in part, because they're rich in spirit – or have to act like they are.

Another common cultural-economics explanation of why artists typically don't make much money is the rampant competition for relatively few gigs: the supply of willing artists vastly outstrips the demand. That's true, but a theory like Abbing's helps explain the baseline desire to make art, even when the artist grows up and loses the rock-star sunglasses.

Plenty of people actively pursuing arts careers know that even considerable success means not much more than a below-average wage, probably supplemented by a lot of art-adjacent activity. They submit to this logic because they see their work as a higher calling.

That may be a delusion of grandeur, but the artist needs the buyer to have the same delusion. It's a defensible delusion, though. Art and artists can act above money because they can trace their roots to the one thing that has always claimed to mean more than money: the divine. The modern artist will only rarely claim to be communing with the gods, but that just means that things have evolved: in considering art a 'calling' or striving to capture some fundamental and inalterable truth, artists show their roots as the people who interpreted the gods. Almost all of the earliest people we would now consider artists, and nearly everything they made that we might talk about as art, worked in service to better understanding the forces that seemed beyond our world. Art was our explanation for things we could not immediately grasp, the creative spirit a mimetic tribute to the unseen, frightfully unknowable forces that shaped us. The first people who got paid for their art were also the first people paid for their services to the gods.

Placing money above art feels like blasphemy because, in some practical sense, it is. Priests aren't supposed to be in it for the money either, and the first artists were essentially priests.

Poetry isn't the oldest art, but it could probably be called the first thing we started to recognize as art, as something similar to decoration, celebration, or communication yet somehow more. There is a reason Aristotle named his work on aesthetics *Poetics.*

The earliest poet we know by name – to the degree that we can be confident she actually wrote what is attributed to her (not a high degree, but then Homer probably wasn't a real person, and no one has trouble giving him credit), is Enheduanna. She was an Akkadian princess and priestess, and both roles had a lot to do with her getting to be a poet. The former role usually means rich parents – in her case, Sargon of Akkad, the guy who created the whole empire – which is still the best and most realistic path to becoming an artist. As for the latter role, there wouldn't have been much distinction between the job descriptions for priestess and poet (although priestess was the only real job): both entailed understanding, interpreting, and paying tribute to the gods. I don't consider myself qualified to comment on the quality of Mesopotamian poetry of the 2300s BCE, so I will simply say that, more than her hymns to the goddess of love, war, fertility, and the temple, her most enduring poetic contribution was her claiming, and declaiming, of her own work: 'The compiler of the tablets was En-hedu-ana. My king, something has been created that no one has created before.' That last part is the root of the prestige artists will subsequently claim: I am able to make something no one else can. By celebrating the gods, she becomes godly herself, creating like they do.

———

For presumably most of our unwritten history, and a fairly significant chunk of what is recorded, artistic creation consisted of creative versions of worship. Our most documented example is found almost two thousand years later, almost two thousand kilometres west of Akkad. If the subjects of Greek poetry and drama weren't solely religious – see: Sappho – the support system most definitely was. Poetry, which was nearly always accompanied by music, was performed most often and with most reward at the numerous festivals to the gods that made up a good chunk of Greek social life. Though Homer was not a participant, the works that bear his name were disseminated by rhapsodists, travelling performers who went from festival to festival, supported variously by temple staff or rich benefactors. Another venue for its performance was symposia, which wealthy men used as something like modern-day book clubs, albeit explicitly about improving the quality of their spiritual life. Beyond recounting the exploits of the gods, poetry was considered to offer instruction on living properly and provide opportunity for self-reflection.

Festival performance evolved into the art form that would support the most working artists in the Mediterranean until Christianity took over the Roman Empire: the theatre. 'Working artists' by the standards of the time, that is: sculptors and painters were littered across the Greek and Roman world, too, but they were only fitfully considered to be doing anything other than manual labour – though their craft also evolved out of what we'd consider religious sentiment, from crude figures to Egyptian death rituals to images of tribute.

According to tradition (or Aristotle, anyway), theatre was invented by Thespis, a sixth-century BCE poet credited as the first person (in Greece, anyway) to perform as someone other than himself (in a written play, anyway). It's where we get the word *thespian*. However solid Thespis's claim really is, the things he was said to be performing – dithyrambs, the stories of gods and heroes (who were usually at least part god) – were almost certainly where theatre began. Performed most famously at Athens' Dionysia, a festival founded sometime around 540 BCE, these evolved from lyrical one-handers, variously incorporating masks, other actors, choruses, a separation of labours, and eventually a place in society that made them one of the central preoccupations of the rich and powerful in the city. As a direct consequence of drama's religious roots, performing and supporting it was seen as offering something greater than just a night at the theatron, as evidenced by the prestige that accompanied footing the bill.

The duty of paying for the production, including everything from the playwright to the costumes, fell to the choregos: rich Athenians appointed by the ruler or some faction in the city to ensure that the show could go on. Lest we think art's roots are significantly purer than its modern practice, bragging was a significant factor: these were competitions, at least from the time when we start having reasonable records of them. Part of what the choregos were paying for was a chance at glory (like executive producers with the Best Picture Oscar, these money men would get their name on the prize, should their play win, though at least the Greeks made them share it with the playwright).

From the thespian's perspective, the competition among the choregos to support celebrated companies was almost as important as the dramatic competition, and the dramatic competition helped attract higher bids. Eventually companies were able to travel throughout the peninsula, sometimes at the invitation of other rich men in other cities, sometimes in hopes that someone would hire them as they were passing through. There's not a lot of solid accounting from the Greek period, but the general sense is that this was a decent enough job to justify an itinerant lifestyle, with some great perks, including feasts in your honour. Many of the playwrights we remember and perform today would have been essentially the artistic directors of these companies. A rare few were able to make a sizable nut – Theodorus, a tragedian, is listed among the donors to a temple at Delphi – but our best indications are that the majority of the company was very much hand-to-mouth.

By the time we reach the period when Western history starts caring more about Rome than Greece, that had changed somewhat, at least partially because theatre drifted further away from religious purpose. Theatre became an essential part of the festivals and games Roman leaders used to keep the public occupied – the back half of *panem et circenses*. By the time we start measuring years in double digits, plays were featured in more than half of all festivals, with rich prizes and solid guarantees attached to them: a performer could take home about half the annual salary of a labourer from just one festival performance, and considerably more if they won any of the burgeoning number of prizes. (Roman festivals did come with slightly more risk than the Greek ones, though: if people really hated what you did, you could be forced to give some of the money back. This made some thespians play more pointedly to the audience.) There was a large disparity – many companies of actors were filled out with slaves – but if things were good, they were very good: there are stories of actors being rewarded with entire stables of horses, and some of them could also earn incredible salaries from side gigs teaching political leaders the art of keeping an audience rapt.

This lucrative professionalism came with its own costs, though. Part of why theatre people could earn a decent wage was the rise of guilds, which negotiated for reasonable pay for everyone involved; for some purists, this represented something like the corporatization of theatre, pulling it out of the higher realms of public service and into the dirty world of common business. And despite the higher wages, being an actor in Roman society came with serious drawbacks: performing onstage incurred the judgment of 'infamia,' which stripped them of some of the basic rights of citizens. In the Roman case, this chiefly meant the right to vote or hold any form of office (Romans had a much more restricted view of who could do those sorts of things than we do). In practice, the biggest hit was to their social reputation, not far off from how modern society might consider, say, a sex worker (more on that in a second). There was a time when actors were technically barred from having relationships with politicians – partially due to their ill repute, though possibly also to the belief that their charisma might warp the political process – not that that seems to have stopped a whole lot of them. Probably the most famous example came in the time of the Byzantine Empire: Justinian I's wife, the empress Theodora. She was born into an acting family and had spent time on the stage; her past didn't stop her from reaching her position, though it did open her up to all manner of rumours and attacks from her and her husband's enemies. The rumours may not have been entirely unwarranted: though there's no real evidence Theodora did it, by the time she became empress in 527 CE, there were a few hundred years of history of women actors in particular using their time onstage as an advertisement for their more lucrative prostitution services – at least part of the reason why the Christian Church cracked down so heavily on theatre, actors, and performance in general when it came to power, almost entirely erasing the link between theatre's religious roots and its role in Christian society for several hundred years.

That was not, however, the end of the connection between the divine and art, even in the areas of the world that Christianity came to dominate. Theatre found its way back in the form of passion plays and other re-enactments of Christian stories; poetry lingered in cloisters; and the need for iconography and visual depictions of Bible stories helped the visual arts develop from craft into full-on art, often at the explicit direction of Church figures. This basic arc is a familiar one throughout the history of art and the gradually expanding definition of 'artist.' The desire to express the ineffable, to grasp at the powers beyond our world, begins as an ancillary to some other activity: priests doing poetry; statuary gradually finding religion. People find ways to directly support it to honour whatever god or philosophy they happen to hold on to. The edifices of commerce get built around this activity: it becomes more specialized, more formalized, and elevated to a particular skill worthy of support that reflects as much on the buyer as on the artist. With all this money and prestige flooding in, the original purpose gets more and more overwhelmed until eventually it's hard to see how the work really fulfills that purpose. Even if the art tries to trade off the claim, people no longer buy it, literally or figuratively; its prestige evaporates, and some other form that feels more closely aligned to those higher ideals begins to flourish in its place.

If people with money could just create art, they wouldn't need to pay someone else to do it. But, crucially, they also need to pay someone who embodies the ideals they're seeking.

From the moment the artist starts cashing in on that reputation, two important things happen. First, other people start looking to cash in on that reputation as well. Second, the artist begins the dance of inevitable decline in their own medium's prestige, clinging to their loftier ideals while constantly bargaining with material realities that render ideals moot. Whatever claims the buyer and the artist are making, material realities are precisely what art is supposed to be above, and so the more they creep in, the further art gets from the ostensible reason it's being bought in the first place. The best time for artists' cultural prestige comes right before the best time for them to make money, which comes right before the best time for other people to start making money off art. In certain ways, getting to call yourself an artist is your compensation for sharing your intangible values for a fraction of tangible value. One of the surest ways we can tell someone is an artist, whether we are Hans Abbing or just a regular old intuitive understander of dynamics, is if a lot of other people are also making money off their art.

Based on the modern conception of artists, though, this is some kind of fair compensation. If you are being recognized for your gift, as opposed to recompensed for your labour, you should be grateful for anything you make, especially if it conveys your glory to some higher power.

So maybe this was always just a very good lie told by people better at making money than making poetry; maybe it only feels true because the deal was struck in art's earliest days. Or because it comforts someone self-aware and creative enough to realize that their chosen path has left them less materially comfortable than they could have been if only they had been less in touch with their sensitive, elevated soul. I'd love to have a definitive answer – for myself as much as for the nice people who have paid between $9 and $25 to track down my thoughts on the matter – but I'm at a loss. What I know for sure is that art is better for you than money, so artists are always going to be beaten by money, because it comes with fewer rules for how you interact with it. Or if not beaten by money, then by the people who know how it works and what it means and what you can do with it. Artists have been sold an idea by people who are necessarily better at selling things. It's possible to take some solace in the fact that this has always been true – but neither solace nor art is likely to pay the rent. There are much better ways to make a living, if not necessarily to live. (But there I go again, falling into the artist's trap of self-flattery; no wonder I can barely make a living.)

The darker implication here is that, if art is ultimately subservient to money, we can't say that it is the higher calling; the meaning we ascribe to art is ultimately dictated by these material ends, and the higher force we are serving is the thing we flatter ourselves into thinking we're above. I don't know if that is something I can really believe; after all, I'm writing books, not working at a hedge fund. But money can hammer down the boundaries of your world whether you're thinking about it or not. Maybe trying to escape that reality through art, instead of meekly submitting to its dire dictates, is the real failure.

Or maybe we artists should be able to find genuine contentment in sharing our gift with the world, because there's no gift the world could directly give us back that would be worth it. I cannot entirely make up my mind whether that's a hopeful attitude or a resigned one. But maybe that's the price of ineffability.

2: 'The Infinite Treasure Granted to Us by Our Creator for Both of Us to Enjoy'
How Patronage Made Artists

Tiziano Vecelli, generally known to us now as the painter Titian, created paintings that earned him veneration in his day and went on to define the Venetian school of the later Italian Renaissance. He was supposedly discovered as a child, when he painted a gorgeous image of the Madonna on a wall in Pieve di Cadore, a backwater hill village 110 kilometres from Venice. These days we know him as one of the Italian Renaissance's, and especially Venice's, towering figures. His versatility, development, and growing notoriety make him an almost perfect avatar of the Renaissance itself.

But the colours in this Madonna were what attracted people at first, especially since he made them himself, from the nectar of local flowers. One of his biographers, Sheila Hale, notes that there are plenty of reasons to assume this is a just-so story, which popped up in biographies even while he was still alive. It encapsulates a little too perfectly his later reputation in a childhood anecdote. He created his own colours, notable because his use of colour was and is one of the defining features of his paintings. He did it as an untrained child, demonstrating some innate, God-given gift. This part wasn't just a common trope in biographies of this time – it was also something of a necessary precursor to justify his presence in royal and papal courts.

Titian spent quite a lot of his career as a court painter: at the time of his death, he was the only person to have painted portraits of both a pope and a Holy Roman Emperor. Anyone who pulled that off would have to have some talent. Whatever gifts from God Titian could claim, though, he also got a lot from quite extensive training, including years carving woodcuts for Venice's new and voluminous publishing industry – at the time he was doing it, Venice accounted for one-sixth of the books produced in Europe – and two apprenticeships, one with the first Italian painter to be knighted, and the other with possibly an uncle but at least a family friend; Titian had a divine gift for making the right connections at every stage of his life.

Getting the support of anyone with political power – the councillors and doge of Venice; Italian dukes; God's representative on earth – didn't come from being a dab hand at mixing pigments. To justify sizable expenses – in Titian's case, his salary from Charles V topped out at about ten times the amount of a skilled artisan, and he got paid extra for each piece he actually produced – he had to be more than just a craftsman. To be worthy of the patronage of a king, let alone a pope, his talent had to flow out from a blessed soul, the proof of his unimpeachable virtue and superior morals; it was, after all, proof of their own divinely granted wisdom and benevolence that they recognized such consecrated virtue and ensured it was well taken care of. It's not clear how much even the monarchs believed this, but it was the Renaissance equivalent of the artist's statement, the proof that you understood your and your art's place in the world: serving at the pleasure of the people paying for it. In addition to talent, God gave Titian a preternatural understanding of this aspect of the work. Upon receiving one of his first major commissions – painting a mural on the Fondaco dei Tedeschi, the city's most important merchant building – he told the council that he didn't even care about the money, he just wanted a lifetime sinecure that essentially let him collect regular fees from the business happening inside, as well as a government-funded studio and two full-time assistants. Because it was all about the work: 'I value nothing more than my own honour, and wish only to have enough on which to live.' That an annual stipend for the rest of his life would have worked out to many, many times the cost of a single painting (and let him do other work on the side, for which he could also be paid) had nothing to do with it, you see. It was only his desire to honour his gift that made him ask.

That particular source of income was cancelled about a year later, after Venice lost a war and a good chunk of the Rialto neighbourhood to fire, but Titian never lost his ability to talk his way into extended support from rich people – nor to find a way to do as little as possible to earn it, while working on other pieces and securing other patrons and commissions. In 1516, he negotiated another sinecure, with similar terms, to paint the Hall of the Great Council. He first used the studio to paint portraits of a healthy portion of Venetian society, including many of the Great Councillors. Whatever Titian's artistic interest in portraiture, it was a fabulously good business decision: his most notable contemporaries, people like Vasari and Michelangelo, dismissed portraiture as a lesser art, which left an opening for ambitious young painters to make bank off rich people's desire to see themselves on canvas. (And he was very good at knowing what rich people's desires were. He once claimed that all great art was due to the wise guidance of the powerful people who commissioned it: 'The more I consider the matter, the more I am convinced that the glory of ancient painting was largely, if not wholly, promoted by these great princes, in that they guided the

artists very wisely, and this later earned them fame and praise.'
Laying it on a little thick there, my man.)

Titian would eventually become the painter of choice for
notables across Italy, beginning with Alfonso d'Este, Duke
of Ferrara, who made him his de facto court painter – de
facto because, though Titian got both regular commissions
and a salary, he was never actually required to live for any
length of time in Ferrara, instead having his travel to and
from Venice covered. A somewhat distant relation of
Alfonso's, Federico Gonzaga, conveniently the ruler of
Mantua, secured a portrait by gifting Titian some farmland,
then did him one better by introducing him to Charles V of
Habsburg, the Holy Roman Emperor. As luck would have it,
Charles was dealing with some of the more violent aspects
of the Protestant Reformation around this time and happened
to need someone who could make him look suitably heroic.
Titian would also become his de facto court painter –
although, again, he stayed in Venice, so reluctant to travel
that he developed a reputation for being able to paint incredible likenesses based solely on descriptions, having never
even seen many of his noble subjects.

Charles V granted Titian so much favour that a similar
sort of folk tale grew up about their relationship: supposedly,
on one of Titian's rare actual visits to court, the Holy Roman
Emperor himself stooped over to pick up the master's fallen
paintbrush. That's probably only a metaphor, but Charles
did grant Titian that very important salary, had him paint
portraits of his most intimate associates – including his son,
his dead wife, and Titian himself – and even knighted him.
(This wasn't an empty honour like modern knighthood: it
allowed Titian to appoint judges and legitimize children, a
perk he took advantage of.) Shortly after Titian was knighted,

twenty-one years after he first took the commission, sinecure, and studio to paint the Great Hall, Venice finally threatened to take it away if he didn't finish the painting, which he had not yet started. Well, at least not in the sense of putting paint on the walls: Titian claimed to have done the sketches. He finished it within the year and held on to that Great Hall position until he died, despite often making many times its annual pay on individual commissions, using his status as Charles's painter to set prices.

It's a bit hard, if we're honest, to untangle an appreciation of Titian's work from the fact that he was the Holy Roman Emperor's portrait guy: there was an awful lot of incentive to appreciate him and his paintings. Even so, Titian's portrait work in particular is still incredibly striking, with a depth and subtlety, especially of colour, that didn't really exist before him. Rubens and Rembrandt both considered him a true inspiration, so it seems fair to say he had a gift, even if it seems less a divine endowment and more like an evolution in painting technique. With all that said, even Titian himself once admitted that his passion was for his 'pensions': the various posts, sinecures, and regular payments that he acquired. What little of his writing or thinking survives is almost all concerned with the business side of his operation. And though his status among Renaissance greats is a matter of opinion, it is an absolute fact that, despite growing up in a backwater hill village, he eventually turned himself into one of the richest and most prosperous non-noble people, let alone artists, in Italy.

Perhaps that did all stem from gifts so divinely abundant that they were evident in a child who could mix his own colours from flowers. I mean, sure, it's not unreasonable to think he had an interest in art that made it seem like a viable career; after all, he left Cadore as a teenager to work in a Venice workshop. But it's just as likely that a family living on the fringes of the richest and most cosmopolitan city in Europe knew a guy in the city whose workshop needed an apprentice and who knew their son needed a job. That that kid became notable enough to inspire legends about his birth is as much as a testament to his ability to convince very powerful people to support him as it is to whatever else God may have given him.

The modern conception of patronage – where, basically, a ruler or rich guy takes it upon themself to directly support an artist, whether by regular commission, salaried support, or both – has its roots in the Renaissance. But the broad idea of being on the payroll of some powerful person or institution while pumping out the occasional painting or poem is, realistically, the dominant method of surviving as an artist for most of human history. This isn't just craven opportunism on the part of the creative spirit. Having the time and resources both to acquire training – anything from simple literacy to technical instruction – and to put it to use required the largesse that accompanies power. (There have also always been people making things we'd consider art explicitly as a living or trade, but they are almost never allowed anything like the status of 'artist.' At best they might get 'artisan,' usually because they are so crass as to need to make money off the stuff they make.)

Under this earlier style of pseudo-patronage, most of the people who did create things were discouraged from claiming any sort of personal, egoistic credit for the work. Anyone who was allowed to sign their name was usually being paid for something else, with artistic recognition a bonus of their already prestigious position. It's partly a mistake of our modern conception that we would even call the things they made 'art' or the people that made them 'artists.' For the people of the time, the artifacts were more properly understood as functional, like wallpaper or record-keeping or, most grandiose of all, offerings to the divine. To whatever degree they contained or conferred any special status, it was due to whoever was paying for them, in the same way that whatever colour you paint your living room reflects on your taste, not the genius of Benjamin Moore.

Often, the unnamed artisans belonged to some kind of religious tradition: most of the religious iconography of medieval Europe, from the stuff on the walls to the illuminated manuscripts, was handled by monks – though it occasionally went to artisans paid by religious officials. Later, as things needed to get grander to be appropriately Godly, the Church ramped up commissioning tradespeople, though it took a while for them to bother to record who did what: for instance, we do not know the original architect of Paris's Notre Dame Cathedral.

This was true for Christendom's neighbours, too. The early Islamic caliphates were a little more open to free inquiry and modes of expression that weren't expressly religious, but anything resembling art tended to be the preserve of skilled craftspeople. We know virtually none of the people who designed monumental buildings like the Umayyad Mosque in Damascus or Hisham's Palace in the West Bank. Nor do we know who created the incredibly intricate mosaics and patterns that decorate them. We are not even sure if they were favoured or recognized in any way by the people who commissioned them – but, of course, we do know those people.

Islamic poets were given the courtesy of having their names remembered, but here again poetry was usually something someone with other connections, if not an outright position of prominence, did in their spare time. Marwan ibn Abi Hafsa is part of what was once called the most poetic family in Islam, as both his father and grandfather served in distinguished courts; Marwan rose to the greatest prominence at least partly because he wrote poetry that was so effusive in his praise of his variously ranked patrons. He was first banned by the ruling caliph, then hired to write in his support, then assassinated by a rival political faction who were unhappy he was making them look bad. Rūmī, the one Arabic poet you know if you don't know Arabic poets, went the opposite route, running a madrassa and taking inspiration from his mystic worship with a Sufi tariqa (Sufism's ecstatic, inward-focused practice, which produced many notable poets, although it generally served as more of a source of creative inspiration and social support than a material source of comfort).

This was usually the case in Europe, as well, although there are an impressive number of pretty renowned 'poets' – notably the author of *Gawain and the Green Knight* – about whom absolutely nothing is known, except sometimes a name and a record or supposition of which courts they served. The Church did produce a number of named poets, although they tended to have pretty limited range, even compared to their Sufi counterparts, sticking primarily to hymns and Bible retellings. A reasonable stand-in for that lot might be the monk Otfrid of Weissenburg, the first poet writing in vernacular German whose name we still know. His major work was the *Evangelienbuch*, a retelling of Jesus' life in rhyming couplets (a full 1,200 years before *Hamilton*).

It was far more common, in Europe, for poets – whether strictly in the written form, or those who also set their lyrics to music – and the odd prose writer to have some form of position in court, frequently as a sort of ambassador to other courts, though they occasionally seemed to have real power. (The modern conception of the troubadour is of an itinerant wanderer with an instrument on his back, but that sort of thing was more likely to be considered minstrelsy, and of such low status that its practitioners were rarely worthy of any note or royal favour.) Most troubadours were members of court who wrote in their spare time, as evidenced by their preoccupation with courtly love and chivalric values. The oldest surviving troubadour songs we have were likely preserved because they were written by William IX, Duke of Aquitaine, who, when he wasn't fiddling around with songs, helped lead the Crusade of 1101.

As for vernacular-language literature, most of its primordial figures were highly placed bureaucrats one or two steps removed from supreme power in their region. Snorri Sturluson, the author of the *Prose Edda*, among other works, was a lawyer, spokesperson for the King of Norway, and lawspeaker of the Icelandic parliament, a position roughly equivalent to a ceremonial monarch (or, if you're Canadian, lieutenant governor) today. Dante was a Florentine politician who was serving as envoy to the pope when he was sent into the exile that eventually produced the *Divine Comedy*. Chaucer held a variety of courtly appointments and was important enough to Edward III that the king paid a ransom to free him after he was captured by French forces in 1360, well before he wrote *Canterbury Tales*. He was at various times apparently rewarded by the royals directly for his poetry – in 1374, Edward III gave him a gallon of wine per day for life in recognition of his literary contributions – but he kept some form of court-adjacent role for more or less the entirety of his life, including acting as foreman for the king's building projects, a member of parliament, and a forester in the royal forest.

———

The absolute peak of this mode of artistry, though, was in Imperial China, roughly contemporary to the people we've talked about above but stretching for several hundred years in either direction. Art was not just a happenstance of enough time and money for training and creation: it was specifically selected for, judged, and celebrated among the scholar-officials who made up the Imperial bureaucracy. Disciplines like painting and poetic composition were explicit criteria in the Confucian exams that granted entry to their position, and those skills were celebrated in the court and among their fellow bureaucrats.

What exactly was emphasized – and exactly how Confucianist the exam and the values it was evaluating were – varied with dynasties and emperors' desires, but even from the earliest days, would-be officials had to demonstrate a knowledge of classic works and an ability to appreciate arts like calligraphy, poetry, and painting. By the time of the Song Dynasty, which lasted from 960 to 1279 CE, the system greatly expanded, and those being examined also had to show evidence of a particular sensitivity and style in writing both prose and poetry, as well as painting. The system was designed to be purely meritocratic, although it was susceptible to the usual thumbs on the usual scales. The ability to create worthy art proved that the people who should be ruling, or at least administrating, over everyone else had suitably enlightened souls. (We have definitely come up with far worse systems for deciding who holds sway over our lives – like, for instance, limiting it to soulless strivers who see no appreciable difference between management consultancy and public service. At a bare minimum, proving that you have the ability to clearly convey a sophisticated understanding of, say, *King Lear* – or, hell, Paul Verhoeven's *Starship Troopers* – doesn't feel like a horrible bar to make people clear.)

These were supposed to be important jobs, directing construction and enforcing royal decrees and generally doing the high-level bureaucratic work you would associate with being the representative of an emperor in a geographic area. But the prolific output of the people whose names survived suggests that they had lots of downtime. It's possible that the sort of people who passed outrageously hard entrance exams were all type-A nutjobs. But the frequency with which they have reputations as drunks, shit-stirrers, and general rapscallions, and the rather loud carping that sneaks into their work and correspondence whenever they actually had a significant amount of work to do, suggests that a lot of these were probably closer to Confucianist email jobs, except the meetings were about who owed pigs to whom.

With the exception of the relatively fewer women who rose to prominence, virtually any Chinese poet, painter, essayist, or scholar of the era studied for years in an attempt to become an official. And the women tended to have intimate connections to the system: Li Qingzhao, one of the most celebrated Chinese poets of all time, was typical only insomuch as she was the daughter of and married to prominent officials, with the access to study and leisure that those connections implied. The result was a flourishing of the arts, not only in sheer production, but in content: Chinese artists – even some of the non-official ones – explored ideas and formal experimentation that wouldn't get solidified in the Western canon for centuries.

One of the purest examples of this is the poet and painter Su Shi, who – fortunately for the purposes of autocorrect – took the pen name Dongpo. Born near the peak of the Song Dynasty, in 1037, he is almost a perfect avatar for what actually constitutes a 'meritocratic' appointment. His father, Su Xun, never did pass the imperial exam, but was from a sufficiently wealthy family that he never had to muddy his soul with much other than study. His devotion to interpreting the classical texts – which included personally instructing his sons in the same – eventually got him recognized and celebrated as a master of the period. For Dongpo's purposes, all that really mattered was that his father was sufficiently regarded by the emperor's inner circle that one of them offered to mentor Dongpo after he passed his Imperial exam at the age of nineteen. (To give you an idea of how big a deal these exams were, both Dongpo and his brother Su Zhe became minor celebrities after passing the exam, on account of their young age and stellar performance.) This didn't immediately lead to a flowering of Dongpo's artistic gifts, but it did get him a high-profile job in Hangzhou, an important enough city that the Imperial capital was moved there in the twelfth century. And, to undercut my own dismissive commentary a little, while there he did oversee the construction of a causeway across that city's West Lake that still exists as a UNESCO World Heritage Site.

Dongpo's most notable works from his early days as an official were a report on the poor economic conditions of the country's iron-producing regions and a series of letters that were elegantly expressive – and sufficiently critical of other officials that he was exiled to a distant, unpaid post in Hubei province. Political exile was art's gain, though: he took his pen name from the small farm he lived on ('eastern slope' is the literal meaning) and produced some of his most recognized poems and paintings. The former were notable for their experimentations in the ci style: lyrics set to existing tunes that, until Dongpo's innovations, were typically sentimental love songs. His style, which eventually became codified as háofàng (literally 'bold') were more philosophical and melancholy, more obsessed with mortality and his own minor failings, often literally drawn from the dissatisfaction he had with this less prestigious period of his life. The poem he wrote on the birth of his son, conveniently titled 'On the Birth of a Son,' is a good example of his general mindset, to say nothing of his opinion of his political opponents:

> Families when a child is born
> Hope it will turn out intelligent.
> I, through intelligence
> Having wrecked my whole life,
> Only hope that the baby will prove
> Ignorant and stupid.
> Then he'll be happy all his days
> And grow into a cabinet minister.

This inner turmoil was also reflected in his paintings. Few of them survive, but they are notable for their attempt to express his feelings through an image, as opposed to merely capturing the image. As a recent Christie's auction of one of his surviving paintings, *Wood and Rock*, noted, 'Su Shi's ideas on what it was to create an image, and the relationship of the image to the internal psychology of the painter, were revolutionary, and can be seen as a launchpad for painting as a non-representational, psychologically driven process.' The auctioneers were trying to sell the thing, but still: he was recognized even in his time for the expressive quality of his brushwork and the way it conveyed what was roiling inside him. Before him, Chinese painting, like the Renaissance masterworks we'll discuss later, tended to derive its meaning more from the choice of subject and the realistic style than from the painter's self-expression.

However bad exile was for Dongpo's official career, it was wonderful for art, giving him both time and a subject matter worthy of his expression. I'm not a great believer that you have to suffer for your art, but it doesn't strike me as unreasonable that a high-ranking official should have to come down a peg or two to make something that really echoes across the centuries.

Dongpo's painting, and in particular the development of a style of interiority made visible, hints at another paradox of the scholar-official system of art. The worthiness of a piece was due foremost to the status of the person who made it, and only once that bar was cleared, its other properties. Chinese artisans were arguably making more sophisticated imagery, creating household goods and even decorative paintings with things like trompe l'oeil and depth techniques that would not show up in officials' paintings for a long time. But these not-quite artists were explicitly excluded – even mocked – by their social betters, primarily because, say it with me now, they were creating those things for the market and not to express the inherent worthiness of their souls.

This wasn't just an aesthetic theory, at least not in China. Confucian ideals are quite clear about the deficient character of anyone who prizes acquiring wealth above developing their inner sensitivities. Though there are certainly worse organizing principles, there wasn't much room for grey areas, like the fact that most artisans were eking out a living, not amassing treasure hordes. This is the great self-justifying myth of meritocratic systems: if these people were truly worthy, had sufficiently sensitive souls, they would have passed their exams and earned salaries from the state. Circular logic is useful for keeping certain people out of the circle.

It gets trickier when you don't have a vast, state-sponsored philosophy to justify the separation of the comfortably refined from the uncouth strivers. In Europe, the people who came to be regarded as patrons and the people who (often somewhat reluctantly) chased that patronage had to spin up a more ad hoc system. They ended up with a more individualist ideology in that they had many dispersed benefactors – but the same basic circular logic prevailed. To make the artists worthy of the money they were paid and the patrons worthy of having the money to dole out, art had to have powerful moral and spiritual implications. This is, in the basest terms, what separates artist from artisan: an artisan can make you a good thing, but an artist will make you a good person. For that, you can justify almost any price.

––––––––––

Today's version of the question 'But is it art?' is a bit of a shell game: it is usually asked about the work of an artist deliberately trying to provoke exactly that question. A closer analogue to Imperial China or Renaissance Europe would be our lower-stakes debates about what constitutes high or low art, the truly edifying and enlightening stuff versus the commercial stuff that is at best a momentary distraction on the way to the grave (maybe call it art vs. entertainment). We've mostly gotten over dismissing entire mediums – not even our modern desiccated high-society husks are going to claim that Wagnerian opera is inherently more worthy than HBO-ian television drama, although new frontiers like video games and social-media personalities may confound us. But the intra-medium argument still runs strong, whether that's painting versus comics, or intellectual cinema versus comic-book movies.

Consider poetry. For basically all of recorded history, it has been granted a rarified status. Part of this is the relative rarity of literacy. Even if any rough-and-tumble swine merchant could have strung together a choice stanza, it was only the educated elite who could preserve it for posterity, and there is nothing historically more worthy of elevation than something the poor and uneducated can't do. But poetry has always had a natural antipode: utilitarian prose concerned with rote record-keeping, the affairs of the state and market, plainly conveying information or an idea. Even elevated forms of this – histories and philosophies, considerations of the purpose of people and gods, eventually prose fiction – were seen to lack the formal constraints, metaphorical language, and inward focus of verse.

Renaissance artists who would come to define the period had to lean into this latter aspect. The visual arts are inherently useful – even a Pollock is ultimately a way to decorate your wall. As increasingly realistic techniques – compositional ones like depth and figure arrangement; practical ones like colour mixing and preservation – came within the grasp of the most basically trained artisan, to be an artist meant to be above the worldly concerns of the workshop grunt, even if you came out of that system. A major part of this involved convincing people with money that you were not interested in doing things for money: that what they were buying was the opportunity to provide an enlightened soul with the chance to express that enlightenment. Surely the only people who would pay for such a thing must be enlightened themselves.

Aristocratic and bureaucratic moonlighters aside, most artistic production prior to the Renaissance, particularly in Europe, would have been done either as religious observance and/or in a workshop, which is to say it would not have been considered artistic. These were rites or craft products. Particular skill or craftsmanship might fetch a higher price – like making furniture now – but there was no particular sense that what was being made had any sort of higher meaning than decoration, and it certainly wasn't the result of some ineffable spark granted by the almighty creator. Painters in Florence, the cradle of the Renaissance, were in the same guild as physicians and apothecaries (pre–Scientific Revolution physicians and apothecaries, at that).

Guilds served many purposes, but, similar to professional associations today, their primary role was to credential their members, set out fair prices and wages, and protect their membership from threats. Even in cities where they weren't the literal governing body – virtually all guilds were located in cities and served only residents of those cities – they could severely punish anyone who attempted to do what they considered their work without their permission. In return, they promised to provide their members with reasonable working-class wages and sometimes organized markets or brokerages where they could sell their work. Most of the artists/artisans at this time would have been connected to a workshop: the vast majority would have been labourers, unknown even to most of the people who bought their work, but if your work consistently stood out, you might eventually lead a workshop of your own, which would entitle you to oversee production and, more importantly, decide how to divvy up the money that came in.

Though plenty of people found local prominence – and even civic or royal commissions – individuals didn't start to transcend this system en masse until the Black Death in the 1340s and '50s. The dying off of up to half the population of Europe had the effect of suppressing the pool of available labour, which in turn meant, according to Martin Warnke's impressive history of the rise of royal patronage, *The Court Artist*, that cities, churches, and royal courts couldn't just find suitable craftsmen in their own backyards. They had to start competing for the best artists. And as soon as someone's salary was no longer strictly tied to their city, the protections and strictures of the guild started to seem more like impediments than help.

No one at the time would have been equipped, practically or spiritually, to make the argument that certain workers should be able to charge (and do) whatever they like if there is sufficient demand for their services. So, in the decades after the plague years, artists and the people who paid them developed ideas about why this particular tranche of people were a special category unto themselves – there's nothing like losing a lot of people to make you start appreciating what makes some of them special. This is the birth of the artist as we understand it today: someone possessed of a vision and talent that makes them stand apart.

Sixty years after the worst of the plague, Jacopo della Quercia, a turn-of-the-fifteenth-century sculptor and architect, tried to explain to city officials in the Italian city of Siena that they wouldn't be able to lure back his contemporary Giovanni da Siena because he was a court architect in Ravenna now, and that was a different sort of job than that of the craftsmen they hired to make their buildings and sculptures. According to Warnke's translation, he told the officials that Giovanni 'is not a master craftsman wielding a trowel, but a talented "inventor" and "engineer" who would be of only temporary use, for he does nothing but give form to things'; essentially, he didn't make anything but ideas, and he wouldn't be pulled out of that to come get his hands dirty. (If you are wondering, yes, della Quercia was essentially arguing that he should also be considered the same sort of rarified genius.)

Nascent aesthetic theories began to develop as well. Cennino Cennini, the court painter of Padua, wrote *A Treatise on Painting* sometime in the early 1400s. It was mostly stuffed with notes on technique, but he began by explaining that painting was among the highest human occupations because it combined the skill of the hand with 'noble imagination': 'It is the stimulus of a noble mind which induces persons to study these arts, made pleasing to them by the love of nature. The intellect delights in invention; and it is nature alone, and the impulse of a great mind, which attracts them.' A key part of this nobility, and arguably the thing that separated it from mere craft, was that it wasn't mercenary work: 'There are some who follow the arts from poverty and necessity; but those who pursue them from love of the art and true nobleness of mind are to be commended above all others.' He likely wrote this book while in a debtor's prison, in the hopes of paying off his debts. Not because he practised what he preached – he just spent more than he was handsomely paid by his courtly patrons.

Cennini's argument was in line with the idea of the 'artes liberales' – yes, that's where we get 'liberal arts' – namely, arts that were worthy of a free and unencumbered man (they were always talking about men in those days), pursued not for material purpose or gain ('artes mechanicae') but for pleasure. Talents in these arts were conferred by God or Nature, depending on your preferred philosophy, and were not the result of training, which was far too worldly, though artists did require it to reach their full expression. Most importantly, as natural talents, they could not be bought or sold; at best, they could only be 'honoured' with donations or gifts – not for the work produced, of course, but as thanks for being able to witness the work of the beautiful soul.

If this notion helped elevate certain artists, it was more crucial as justification for the extravagant sums that patrons would lay out: their positions, too, were due to the favour of either God or Nature, and everything they did had to be seen as appropriately honourable (though that didn't stop them from doing what they liked most of the time). It was a harmonious cycle of two honourable people honouring each other with their honourable gifts. One person gifted art, the other gifted things like a courtier's salary, a place to live, assistants, studios, supplies, clothes, meals.

Of course, the patrons had more practical reasons for needing good artists around, too. Painting in particular became a valuable diplomatic tool as a gift or if you needed to get a good look at potential matches for your marriable offspring. Giorgio Vasari, the godfather of art history, claimed that canvas became the dominant thing to paint on because it was so easy to transport when the wealthy needed to honour one another with gifts.

Serving both sides of the equation as well as it did, this notion of the artist quickly spread. As Warnke notes, Antonio, the bishop of Florence in the early 1400s, instructed his priests that, when it came time to commission works to adorn their churches, '[t]he painters demand, fairly reasonably, to be paid not according to the quantity of their work, but rather according to their diligence and superior experience.' The archetype and path to glory, now so clearly laid out, did not take long to become polluted. It was widely held among artists that patronage appointments were barely worth the money: they might come with security and more artistic freedom than having to sell your stuff to the masses, but the obligations to noble society were a relentless drag, and patrons could not always be talked into sharing the artist's vision. In-demand artists often sought terms ensuring they would have to be in the vicinity of their patrons as little as possible.

Even when they couldn't dictate terms, artists found other ways to underline their new place in the world. According to Warnke, sixteenth-century Florentine goldsmith, sculptor, and extravagant bullshitter Benvenuto Cellini – one of the first artists to cash in with a wild autobiography – is said to have insulted a chamberlain in the French court by noting, 'Perhaps only one of my kind walked the earth, while a dozen of [your] kind walked in and out of every door.' This kind of behaviour didn't go unnoticed by the patrons: Francis I, tired of Cellini's ego, is said to have told him, 'You … clever as you are, refuse to recognize that you cannot display your talents by yourselves, and that you can only demonstrate your greatness when we give you the opportunity.'

So after only one generation or so was raised with the explicit idea that artists were special, artists started dismissing the people using that idea to justify paying them. However far the practice of art has advanced since then, that aspect has been remarkably consistent.

———————

Though the term has persisted, patronage in its original, purest form began to die with the Enlightenment and its attendant social shifts. These were mostly marginal, incremental changes, but they slowly chipped away at prominent individuals' ability and obligation to make grand shows of their refined taste. The fracturing of the Catholic Church – which saw several of its offshoots take a turn toward a more austere and humble form of worship – made Church support less consistent across the continent, eliminated a potential pool of talent, and left less fat around for grandiose projects in Rome. The consolidation of city-states and regions into wider polities decreased competition for prestige, and a growing sense of nationalism made it less tenable to pay foreigners to hang around making grand works. Imperialist projects demanded resources and altered what was considered impressive: plenty of modern museums, most notably the British Museum, but even places like St. Petersburg's Kunstkamera and Madrid's Museo del Prado, were founded by royals as 'cabinets of curiosities' to show off treasures collected from around the world, only later incorporating or founding separate institutions for what they would consider contemporary art. Most notably, the slow death of the feudal system spread money around a little bit more, making personal patronage slightly less tenable but giving non-hereditary nobility the means to support artists through the market – or to commission single works directly, without the burden of supporting all of an artist's endeavours.

Those two activities essentially capture the role of the modern patron. Some of the most celebrated recent-ish patrons were aristocratic or fabulously wealthy women who didn't really put anyone on the payroll but nurtured entire artistic scenes by hosting salons, gatherings, and displays, and might help out an artist with a place to stay or a timely loan or purchase. Lady Ottoline Morrell, the free-loving inspiration for Lady Chatterley and at least a half-dozen other early twentieth-century novel characters, supported and hosted the Bloomsbury Group, providing money and space for, among others, Aldous Huxley, T. S. Eliot, D. H. Lawrence, the painter Dora Carrington, and philosopher Bertrand Russell (and had lengthy affairs with the latter two). A'Lelia Walker was apparently more chaste, but she was the financial centre of the Harlem Renaissance, hosting parties so regularly that she turned a full floor of her home into a venue, the Dark Tower. Langston Hughes called her death essentially the end of the era.

One of the exemplars for what patrons would become was Peggy Guggenheim, of *those* Guggenheims. Though she did not found most of the museums that bear the name – she started the one that's named after her, but the rest owe their existence to her uncle's foundation – she did provide plenty of their early collections. A collector with enough money to make or break an artist's career, she was introduced to the art world by no less than Marcel Duchamp. Between a foray as a gallerist and opening the Peggy Guggenheim Collection in Venice, she bought enough abstract, surrealist, and cubist art to fill several museums around the world. Her personal connection to the artists never really went beyond friendship and affairs – and I swear I am not trying to make any insinuations about the kind of women who became patrons, but in her own biography she claims to have slept with more than one thousand men in Europe alone. She didn't really support artists in the creation of art, but certainly provided a tremendous boost to their careers.

And that is basically the role of the individual patron today (the buying in bulk, not the fucking, although I'm sure that still happens plenty). Even as prestigious a group as the Art Basel Global Patrons Council is basically a list of people who buy enough art to create markets by themselves. Commissions or promises to buy anything an artist produces do happen at various levels – one such promise from Charles Saatchi to Damien Hirst is what gave us *The Physical Impossibility of Death in the Mind of Someone Living*, that shark floating in formaldehyde – but these generally only come after an artist has reached a certain (demonstrably investable) level, and again there is no formal relationship of any kind here: the patron gets whatever prestige accrues simply from owning the artwork and its attendant resale value, not from supporting the artist differently from someone else with an equal-sized pocketbook.

Some enterprising individuals have tried to revive something like the old model. In the mid-2010s, former film producer/still-wealthy scion Stefan Simchowitz began to make a name for himself in Los Angeles as a rather prodigious supporter of young up-and-coming visual artists. Part of what separated him from other eager-eyed gallerists and collectors was his willingness to directly fund the artists' living expenses, paying for studio space and supplies but also covering rent, medical bills, and walking-around money. Not precisely villas in Florence, these were nevertheless private supports virtually unheard of for almost any artist, let alone ones who had yet to even have solo shows. He was especially attracted to artists who played well on, and were deeply infected by, the internet, including Petra Cortright (at the time of her association, she was doing somewhat kitschy digital landscapes and abstract pieces on aluminum), Parker Ito (paintings that tend to look like teenagers' bedroom collages), and Kour Pour (slightly ironic paintings of Persian rugs).

The other thing that separated Simchowitz from most other art-world types was a craven promotional style that ran from the maybe generationally innovative (he was a prodigious Instagrammer in the early days of the platform, when most galleries would still kick you out for trying to take pictures with your phone) to the brazenly unethical: he would lay claim to virtually everything made by these young and not-overflowing-with-options artists and then allegedly use his celebrity and business world connections to flip them back and forth, pumping up their value in a way that benefitted him but not so much the artist. Even if these accusations are true, they're a bit rich coming from a wider collective that has plenty of people who view art as nothing but a unique investment instrument. But virtually every artist he worked with has since disavowed him. Such are the people who practise personal patronage these days.

There is, of course, one notable exception: groups that fund art for stated reasons that have to do with promoting enlightened values and giving artists the freedom to explore their work, while pretty obviously also hoping that some of that glory and goodwill reflects back on them. These are the people who give grants. And from foundation to government, their processes are quite different, but the overarching goal remains the same: there's no better way to secure your legacy than to pay an artist to help make it for you.

3: Contributing to the Vibrancy of a Creative and Diverse Arts and Literary Scene
Public Money and How Governments Justify It

In a certain sense, I have been an employee of the Canadian government for the roughly eighteen months during which I wrote this book. Not in the sense of having job security or benefits or a pension contribution or a direct supervisor or a specific place to be or a title, but who's to say that those are what make a job (neither Uber nor the *New York Times* offers them). In the important sense, though – the sense where they give me money and I provide them with tangible proof that I have been working along the parameters we agreed upon when I started – I'm basically a bureaucrat for good words, arranged intelligently. Because the bulk of the money that I have seen for this book – and, if we are to be realistic, will ever see for this book – comes directly from the Canadian government.

(In the spirit of the convention that every project that cashes a cheque from the government is required by the terms of the agreement to note that fact in a prominent place, I also want to note that my money was very specifically from *the* Canadian government – or anyway, its arm's-length granting body, the Canada Council for the Arts – not governments within Canada: Edmonton's government determined my brand of non-fiction was sufficiently non-artistic not to warrant support, while Alberta's government said it seemed fine but wasn't better than other similarly timed projects. To the degree that my motivation for creating anything is fuelled by spite, I do take some small pleasure in the fact that, since my grant came from the highest order of government, the fine people of Edmonton and Alberta had to support my vision regardless of what their blinkered and hateful appointed representatives thought of my work. But then again, this is not equal to the pleasure that could have been derived from them giving me between $5,000 and $20,000, which could have prevented this whole unfortunate aside.)

If there is some particular way to feel about that, I choose solidarity. Though it's certainly not the case in terms of raw dollar amounts – not even the actual bureaucrats and administrators who shepherd these programs are pulling in hundreds of millions in compensation and bonuses, let alone stock options – in terms of actual number and geographic distribution of artists supported by it, government money is the current reigning world champion of keeping artists from literally starving. This is without getting cute with our borders: I am not counting novelists pulling pogey as a writer's retreat or the trickling implications of who exactly is paying for a tenured fine arts professor's salary when you get right down to it. In terms of direct, purposeful transfer, arts funding is propping up an egregious amount of artistic activity. And the vast majority of that funding comes in the form of grants.

If you know someone who is not a household name but seems to be making a go of it as an artist, they are likely in whole or in part living at the grace of government-connected grants, whether from an arts council, a ministry of culture, or just the good old-fashioned tax break for charitable givings. If they are employed in any art form recognized as such when the Habsburgs were still a dynasty, or any kind of performing art that does not end up on multiplex or arena screens, then no matter what they say or what their personal background is, their career – from the buildings they need to access to their probably inadequate salary – is almost entirely thanks to government subsidy. Here in Canada – though pretty much equally in any country that cannot rely on its status as the unquestioned global hegemon to lightly force its cultural projects down the throat of the available public – that is also true of the printed word and a hefty chunk of words broadcast in any form. Even if an artist can afford to turn up their nose at it, the entire structure that allows them to show, see, and otherwise participate in the arts is so enmeshed with government money that rejecting it individually is as meaningless as refusing to eat Madagascar vanilla to help with your carbon footprint. The world is still on fire, except in this case the fire is hot, hot taxpayer funds going to someone else's modern horror clown theatre experiment. The only art forms not substantially propped up by grants, breaks, and occasional infrastructure and event funding are those that have not yet successfully convinced the world they are, properly, arts. (Don't worry, their time will come.)

———————

The question of what exactly constitutes art is as perpetual and elusive for granting bodies as it is in general, and it remains downstream of the larger issue: Why should the creation of art receive any public money?

Truth be told, neither democratic nor modern autocratic governments had much of an issue picking up the torch from their monarchic/oligarchic/aristocratic forebears; they just had a marked tendency to let their ancestors' decisions do most of the thinking for them. Most early forays into government-funded arts initiatives were acts of preservation and documentation, not inspiration: governments were not so much picking winners as robbing the nicest graves.

One of the first things democratic-ish nations did was found things like national museums, galleries, and libraries. To the degree that these symbolized the overall importance of some level of artistic activity, somewhere, they would not even constitute a decent pension for the people actually involved in creating anything. Though most of our institutions are now at least a little bit better about collecting works that are actually being made – the Library of Congress has (or at least had) a Twitter archive, for instance – the historical bias has been toward works well beyond debates about whether they constitute art, and even whether the works in question are worthy examples of their genre. When a body of work has reached the level of appearing in official government collections, it is not only likely that the artist is well beyond basic material concerns, they're frequently dead.

Another important aspect of the institutional project is projecting the right kind of ideas about your nation. A universally acclaimed genius glorifies the achievements of your people; better yet is a universally acclaimed genius who can't offer any pushback on how you're using their legacy. Drafting off existing acclaim, as opposed to helping create it, makes it easier to omit any narratives or tendencies that might weaken the nationalistic case – you can pick your story and then pick the things that fit it – and makes it harder for living artists to actually make a living. Competing with dead geniuses for money and acclaim is hardly a fair fight, and by the time that level of recognition reaches you, you've found other ways to get by. Artists don't get a lot from being trapped behind glass.

———

For governments, starting to replace the patrons who created the concept of artists was a trickier process. The modern government arts funding system – which took it upon itself to make sure art was being made, not just remembered – had to do a delicate dance around classical liberal laissez-faire-ism, budding nationalism, Cold War posturing, the brief rise of a social support system, aristocratic noblesse oblige, and the earth-shaking realities of art in an age of mechanical reproduction – before it ultimately arrived at the same solution the rich and royals had a few centuries earlier, but with more public justification. And it might not have ever got started if a little world war hadn't made it nigh impossible to hear even the simplest symphony in London for a few years.

Well, a little world war and maybe a Great Depression. Contemporary arts granting systems almost universally (if not always admittedly) trace their lineage back to the United Kingdom's Council for the Encouragement of Music and the Arts (CEMA), founded in the midst of the Blitz. With London's symphonies, theatres, and galleries destroyed or under threat of destruction, little in the way of cultural life was flourishing. CEMA was set up to support 'preservation in wartime of the highest standards in the arts of music, drama and painting' through the 'widespread provision of opportunities for hearing good music and the enjoyment of the arts generally' – a suitably stuffy way of saying they were going to give artists some money to make art, because artists didn't have a lot of other ways to get any.

Where the Depression may come in is that CEMA's stated purpose was almost precisely the same as those of the United States' New Deal artist support programs, collectively known as Federal Project Number One. That purpose, as eloquently captured by Secretary of Commerce and New

Deal administrator Harry Hopkins, was 'Hell, [artists] have got to eat, too.' Not so highfalutin as the British justification, and perhaps not so much an arts program as an anti-starvation one, Federal One nevertheless gave some forty thousand writers, painters, musicians, and actors $27 million of the $4.88 billion allocated for public works projects. Beneficiaries included Ralph Ellison, John Cheever, Zora Neale Hurston, a pretty good chunk of the abstract expressionists, Doris Humphrey, Clifford Odets, and Orson Welles.

It's hard to draw direct connections between the New Deal programs and CEMA, though, in part because one of Federal One's main legacies was giving the House Un-American Activities Committee a practice run on how to ruin artists' careers by implying they were filthy communists. A lot of HUAC's red-baiting in this period was a thinly veiled excuse for conservative elements of the U.S. Congress to poison the well against any public funding for the arts whatsoever, which they quite successfully did for at least a generation after. (Some of it was also, of course, racism.) Thanks in no small part to politicians who told artists to grab picks and shovels, all the New Deal programs were shuttered by 1939, and nothing of comparable scope has ever been tried in the United States – or, honestly, any non-communist country – again. (Something similar was suggested for the COVID pandemic, which, given the paucity of the general response to the COVID pandemic in the United States, is – well, artists are supposed to be dreamers, I guess.)

In the United Kingdom of Great Britain in 1941, the conservative cultural force most menacing to those in favour of arts funding was the Luftwaffe, so they weren't overly concerned about not repeating American mistakes. And the U.K. of 1941 would not have credited America with cultural inspiration even if John Philip Sousa marches turned out to be the key to the Enigma machine. Even so, though this does not appear anywhere in official documentation, an emergency fund to help artists feed themselves may have drawn some proof of concept from what had just wrapped up across the pond. Especially since one of CEMA's architects, administrators, and eventual chairs was John Maynard Keynes, whose interventionist theories of economic management had helped craft the New Deal.

Keynes's status as the leading economic mind of the mid-twentieth century was crucial to convincing the people in charge that spending money, even on something as frivolous as a cellist, was basically fine. He was also a long-time patron of the arts – or anyway, a certain sort of art. A central figure in the Bloomsbury Group (and a particular enthusiast of its penchants for analytic philosophy and liberal sexuality), Keynes married Russian ballerina Lydia Lopokova and used his steadily amassing fortune to support institutions like the Cambridge Arts Theatre, the Sadler's Wells ballet company, and the Royal Opera House.

The latter two would also be among the largest recipients of both CEMA and Arts Council funding, when such things came into existence. This was certainly Keynes playing favourites, but he had an edifice of elite cultural opinion to provide him cover. The proximate cause of British arts funding was seeing artists through the war, but its deeper justification was the bubbling consternation that the more worthy elements of British culture were at risk of disappearing, their status and economic health being undermined by an underappreciative public all but hypnotized by crass, unedifying – which is to say Americanized – mass culture.

We've now had at least eighty years of this broad argument, but in the 1930s and '40s it was some of the freshest cultural chatter you could muster among the social set whose status and land holdings were insulated from the Great Depression. Resting on the twin pillars of elite arts discourse – being able to express concern and appreciation for art without actually having to understand it – it was, if not misguided, at least a misapprehension.

New modes of cultural production and consumption were, of course, emerging: photography (both still and motion), phonographs, and paperbacks were all invented in the 1800s but started to flourish as industrial practices made them even easier and more efficient to manufacture and distribute in the early 1900s. Still, their effects had far more to do with the intrinsic qualities of mechanical reproduction than anything notably American, even if the tools, notable practitioners, and efficient distribution systems were often born in America. Most relevant to the people who made the art, though, you were strictly necessary only for its initial creation (after which you would have to find some other job, unless you managed to cut a deal with whoever was documenting that creation), but the resulting art could then be reproduced and shared almost infinitely. This had been the case for writing for a long while (though the early half of the twentieth century saw the rise of easier global trade that spread particular works further), but now this reality extended into arts that had always been social events, intertwined with the status and identity of patrons and audiences. The ability to capture movement and sound turned performing arts into recorded ones, which grossly altered the equation of who and how many were able to make a living off performing. Now the impetus to support those performers wasn't so much what they produced as who consumed it and why.

Besides any military threat, a country like Great Britain was bumping up against the reality that its national culture was not only at risk of failing to be a dominant global one: it could be undermined by some other nation's culture. This was an existential threat. Whatever you might think about the relevance of political boundaries to the greater human condition, the nut of the idea here is basically true: who 'we' are, whatever the we, is pretty tightly wrapped up in our stories about ourselves, our myths and ideas expressed in whatever arts happen to have sufficient public attention. Even if our national character is found in statues of generals, it isn't the military that chisels the stone. By the mid-twentieth century, in places like the United Kingdom, this kind of mythmaking had gotten a little more subtle – less 'we won a battle' and more 'who else but us could produce such refined and thoughtful celebrations of human creativity and sensitivity' – but it had also gotten significantly more diluted. A lot of that good, local, unifying art was not only less reliably accessible, it was being undermined by other art, art that didn't just come from abroad but had a business model, like film. It could first undercut and then obliterate forms that had to do crazy things like pay some or all of the actors, singers, dancers, musicians, directors, composers, stagehands, costumers, technical crew, and ticket takers repeatedly – as in, for every performance.

In England, the nervousness about this outsourcing of cultural production – and the attendant perception of waning cultural superiority – first showed its head not so much in grants as government-supported institutions. The BBC and the British Film Institute were formed, in part, to provide nascent national industries with the space and time to compete against the American versions already significantly outpacing them. Drafting off the same mass-distribution economics, these institutions could create things that, if not fully self-sustaining, attracted enough popular support that they didn't require constant, excruciating justification. The ballets and operas that Keynes and his more bougie/aristocratic contemporaries funded had no way to scale quite to that degree – private support did trickle in, but it allowed only the biggest, most prestigious companies to make ends meet. You will note that those *also* ended up getting government support; part of the justification was that they were doing the worthiest work (and the most readily marketable and capitalizable, but that was omitted from the official story); it doesn't hurt to have the same people giving you private money also be in charge of doling out public money. Though the purse strings are more diffuse and require more public argument to untie, this was not a revolution in public concern for the art so much as a slightly modern spin on the same overlays of networks and personal glories that a previous generation of royals used: we're here to save 'art,' and it just so happens we're friends with all the best artists.

That the coat of nationalism is hiding aristocratic sentiments becomes more apparent when the idea of publicly administered grants starts spreading, particularly through the Commonwealth. Northern Ireland, which inherited CEMA from its overlords in 1943 and was obviously vastly more concerned with an internal enemy than an external one, slapped the paint on especially thick. Until the Troubles, all grant funding came with the stipulation that 'God Save the Queen' must be played before any public performance. As the question of Irish sovereignty grew ever more car-bomby in the 1960s and '70s, that funding favoured work that held a mirror up to society – but only the parts of society that had nothing whatsoever to say about the political situation: nothing with a hint of outward relevance to the issues that were dominating life at the time, or any traditional Irish arts. For a period, the money went only to the largest professional organizations, which the funding body de facto, and in a few cases literally, controlled at an administrative level.

The issues of nationalistic pageantry, elitist control, and concern over the commercialization/Americanization of the arts found their purest expression in the country that has been forced to confront the existential threat of becoming American since before it was even a country: Canada. For Canada – not terribly worried, at the time, about competing narratives from its Indigenous population, our colonial project having eliminated that possibility a century earlier – the question of a national culture was how to create one.

In the mid-twentieth century, as the question of government funding for the arts started to bubble up, it's hard to overstate how little culture that could be considered Canadian there actually was, or how little of it was consumed with any vigour by Canadians. The Massey Commission, formed in part to study the question of funding for arts – it was also, more importantly to the government of the day, tasked with figuring out post-secondary funding – surveyed a landscape that was truly dire. It received written and oral testimony from arts and cultural organizations across the country, and the consequent list of facts and anecdotes could be easily repurposed into a series of devastating one-liners about the health of a cultural industry. The commission heard that Canada's National Gallery was in one tiny wing of what was then known as Canada's National Museum, and its annual funding was outdone by the Chicago Natural History Museum. It was pointed out that, in more than one year during the 1940s, the entirety of the Candian publishing industry had managed to put out twelve novels written in English by Canadian authors, making an English-language Canadian novelist literally one in a million. The Book Publishers wing of the Toronto Board of Trade noted that, per capita, Canada consumed more foreign books and periodicals than any other nation on earth. Theatre companies admitted they would not advertise that plays were of Canadian origin, because audiences wouldn't bother buying tickets.

There are a few reasons to doubt the absolute bleakness of this testimony. For one, it was given almost exclusively by organized societies that were very actively trying to get government money for their causes, and they knew their audience. The Massey Commission was named after its chair, Vincent Massey, eventually Canada's first native-born Governor General, and meanwhile the closest thing Canada had to an aristocrat: scion of a farming equipment dynasty, former high commissioner to London, and, most relevant, occasional writer of jeremiads about the threat posed by American culture on Canada, including 1948's *On Being Canadian*, which came out shortly before he took on the lead role in the commission. As far as the arts were concerned, Massey believed two things. First, he was firmly committed to the secular-humanist idea that the arts were among the chief edifying forces of contemporary life: he described the commission as being 'concerned with nothing less than the spiritual foundations of our natural life.' Equally, he wanted to ensure that Canada maintained and expanded upon its distinct identity. Well, distinct from America, anyway; he was enough of an anglophile to have been a trustee at both Tate and the British National Gallery.

As with his patrician English contemporaries, he knew the only way this could reasonably be achieved was with state intervention – and he knew what sort of art should be preserved. As Paul Litt described it in his 1992 history *Muses, Masses and the Massey Commission*, Massey oversaw a group that 'represented a reactionary elitism geared towards preserving the establishment culture and values of a bygone day in a new era of cultural pluralism.' This was the country's elite codifying the trappings of their social class as the national interest; as Litt later points out, 'Most of the commissioners were friends-of-government insiders who belonged to the same quasi-academic cultural elite and were more concerned about national culture than the arts per se.'

This was reflected in the form the Canada Council for the Arts eventually took. The Massey Commission came out strongly for some form of public subsidy, but the concept was controversial enough that it took eight years and the windfall estate taxes from a pair of Canadian industrialists for things to take shape. Once the money was flowing, though, it flowed overwhelmingly to well-established artists and especially to well-established institutions; until the turn of the millennium, arts funding in Canada was split about 80–20 in favour of organizations, which in addition to supporting artists also had a tendency to support sizable administrations. It was, in short, as much a broad industrial subsidy as an arts program.

However one may feel about the fairness of that particular set-up – and the Canada Council has since worked to change it: since 2017, it's been much closer to a 55–45 split in favour of the big organizations – it did solidify a homegrown industry, even if it did not change the majority of Canadians' level of excitement about explicitly Canadian content. From the land of twelve novelists, there are now roughly two hundred thousand people, according to government employment surveys, who primarily spend their time making some form of art. The Canada Council funded only 1,125 major projects last year, so it's fair to assume that a pretty good number of those people have found some way to do it without cashing government cheques, or anyway, without *only* cashing government cheques.

At the risk of looking my own gift horse too squarely in the mouth, the degree to which this program actually works is a bit harder to establish. By the measure of how many people in the country are able to piece together a living as artists, the Canada Council has done its job. Not only are artists able to sustain entire careers, there exist artists who don't even need to directly access the funding to get buoyed by it: they get by with their artistic or sideline outputs, while the galleries or book publishers or film equipment rental companies they use pay their bills with both direct and downstream grant money. There is some market and appetite for Canadian creations, and so a meaningful tranche of people can devote themselves entirely to creating Canadian culture. As industrial policy, it's hard to argue with government grants: they do sustain industries that artists rely on in all sorts of ways, even if these artists never fill out a grant application themselves.

By the Massey Commission's own logic, and the de facto stance of the Canada Council to this day, things are far murkier. The goal was not only to have more artists working, it was to build a distinctly Canadian culture, in particular one that could withstand the overwhelming cultural assault from the United States. I don't know to what degree that would have been possible, but it plainly hasn't worked. Canada bleeds potential artists to the U.S. at staggering rates – or did from the time of the founding of the Canada Council to the second Trump term – and true financial independence in our country often relies significantly on cracking through in that market, even if you physically stay within our borders. All of our most popular art forms (TV, film, popular music), even the ones we're directly subsidizing, were effectively invented by Americans; even the ones that weren't (theatre, classical music, dance) are dominated by Americans to such a degree that most of what we interact with is created by Americans, even if it's actually performed or portrayed by Canadians.

The esteem for Canadian art among the general public has not appreciably improved, even if we do have a few more cultural icons we can cling to (cultural icons who, outside maybe Gord Downie and Québécois culture, largely earned that reputation beyond our borders). The best that can be said is that art made by and for Canadians has not been wiped off the map. Perhaps that's the best we could have hoped for, but it still leaves us a branch plant, even in our artistic endeavours. Maybe we'll get better at it as our neighbour declines and we try to find ways to define ourselves beyond just opposition to it. In the meantime, I guess, the prospects of being a Canadian artist are a bit better now than in the late 1940s, though we may not be any further ahead on figuring out exactly why the 'Canadian' part of that term is expressly relevant. Unless you're filing out a grant application, of course.

———————

The origin of a thing isn't necessarily its truth. To whatever extent nationalist drum-beating is part of the unspoken logic that justifies continued support of the arts, the practical concern of artists – and, by and large, the panels and bodies that distribute the money – is making sure we can all keep getting by. It should go without saying that, like virtually every artist I know who has received some form of government grant, I'm not particularly driven by enhancing Canadian cultural prestige. I suppose in a certain way I am trying to foster an understanding of a unique Canadian identity, although only in the oblique sense of trying to understand general human culture with the limitations and perspectives of someone who has lived in the country my entire life. (And I should hope it is extremely obvious to any future granting authority that, despite what I have said here, my true beliefs are whatever I wrote in the application, especially if fervent patriotism is now an important consideration.) All of which is to say that, practically speaking, I'm not currently too fussed about why the money is there, I just need it if I'm going to keep doing this.

Even in that slightly flippant attitude, there's a fair bit to unpack. Let's begin with the matter of practicality: as fraught as it might be to secure funding for the arts, it is harder still to figure out what counts as art, which in this case means which creative avenues might be worthy of government funding. The original granters had it relatively easy. They were staring at a landscape of activity that had long ago convinced everyone it was art and was simply in need of some funding to help it survive in a time when models were shifting. Once things are recognized as art, they never really lose that designation: maybe they're dismissed as annoyingly highbrow or out of touch or dead, but they're not not-art. Preservation is a matter of economics, not philosophy, which is a big reason why grants of all kinds tend toward conservative definitions: essentially, an artist is someone who is doing what someone else we see as an artist is doing.

———

Still, conservative doesn't mean static. There are always new practices or forms that can be roped in with previously established art-making. In Canada, for instance, there's been a recent push to more explicitly recognize Indigenous understandings of creation – or, slightly more accurately, Indigenous explanations for why that creation is worthy of broader public support. To some degree, this is correcting for a system that did not so much overlook those understandings as purposefully exclude and destroy them: I'm not an art theorist, but the difference between a ceramicist's pottery and a beadwork earring seems to be a matter of the cultural tradition you have been practising in (call it art school vs. traditional teachings), and it's easy to see why government funding should find it hard to distinguish them. Although even that belies a larger point: some of the effort to level this playing field is a result of a shifting of the political project. Indigenous arts get to be arts because they have now been deemed to fit within the identity Canada wants to project (the impetus and sincerity of that projection is another matter – moral reckoning vs. 'please stop pointing out all the racism' – but at least the money spends).

To bring slightly less baggage to the example, there's also my scenario. I have been rejected from grant funding for this book and had people explicitly tell me not to bother applying for grants because my style of writing is insufficiently artistic.

Personal umbrage aside, I am but a data point in a much wider conversation about which kinds of non-fiction writing qualify as art and which ones, even if they're not purely technical or educational, are still more than a few passages of scintillating prose away from funding.

To spare you a lot of decidedly unscintillating prose, and levels of pettiness I cannot even reach sarcastically, the debate seems to boil down to the level of memoir interwoven into the narrative: a history of using rivers for trade and travel is pure information, whereas the story of how your canoe trip retraced the route of your coureur de bois ancestor and helped you connect with your dead father is art. A book-length exploration of how climate change is affecting river communities, including the one you grew up in: edge case. Can you try to frame it in some way around your own profound awakening?

To bring in more anecdotal experience – which maybe hurts my rhetorical case (but should help my artistic one) – at least some of this seems to be tied to the increasingly out-of-touch belief that artistic funding should be reserved for the free spirits unencumbered by objective factual considerations. Because there are plenty of other funding sources for more prosaic research projects, which, speaking only as a person with a background in journalism, I can say is … [chokes on depression]. Now, obviously I was able to snow one funder with my gift for words and promise to include an unspecified amount of personal anecdote, but the point is that even established mediums can be subject to the whims of individual boards and granting bodies.

Having a recognized medium is only half the battle. Virtually every grant, even if it's explicitly pitched to the delicately titled 'emerging' artist, requires a fairly substantial investment of time and, by implication, resources well before anyone even begins an application. For our emerging friends, that is going to be something like a specific degree, almost certainly post-secondary if not outright graduate-level. Unless you have an absolutely knockout reference from a professor or artist with a pretty direct connection to the degree-granting body – personal connections are explicitly guarded against in public grants, but it's a lot easier to fudge if the funding is private – you will need not just a portfolio but also some proof that someone somewhere other than your school thinks your work is worth something: a group show, publication in a literary magazine, choreography or performance for some other company. But not too much, because then you're not emerging anymore, and you have to compete with the regular artists.

Standard artist grants might require less explicit credentials in exchange for more proof of work. And the work may have to be clearly related to what you're claiming you're going to do, unless the grant promotes 'exploration' or skill-building – and that usually means a different technique or subject, not a medium. Someone who is primarily a photographer is going to be hard-pressed to get their series of paintings funded, let alone a book that's primarily words (well, maybe a memoir), unless they've been consistently showing and publishing in those mediums, too. Prior to my first book, I had about fifteen years' experience writing journalism, criticism, and essays, most of which could easily be described as literary in both intent and venue – most of it for national publications – and I was politely but pointedly discouraged from applying for most grants, since my experience was professional but not, you know, the right kind of professional. It was only after researching, writing, and publishing my first book that I would even be considered for a grant. (I have stopped even asking about my potential for being supported for any kind of fiction. It's my understanding that non-government grants tend to be a little more liberal with their definitions, as they're more often down to the whims of the foundations who give them out, but I'll also cop to a certain self-sabotaging discomfort with taking someone else's money for something I haven't technically proven I can pull off yet, however confident I am in my abilities.)

Now, as hoops to jump through go, even I wouldn't call these grossly unfair: anyone can claim they're anything, and given the rather restricted pool of funding, it makes plenty of sense to ensure the person you're giving money to can prove that they can and will do the thing they're getting money for, to say nothing of establishing that someone other than them thinks they have some merit or talent for what they're making. But these hoops take money and time to clear well before any money is distributed; even to the degree that grants seem like some kind of wasteful public largesse, they are as much a laurel for making it this far as they are a meaningful support system.

Which brings me to the back end of that sentence, about what I 'need' to 'keep doing this.' Having wiggled my way through all the necessary qualifications, and then written an absolute banger of an application, I was awarded just shy of $25,000 by the Canadian government to complete this book – $24,808, to be exact, which was the submitted number because I thought it made my calculations look more honest. At the time, $25,000 was the maximum amount an individual could get for one piece of work; it has since been raised to $60,000. Though you can combine grants from multiple funding bodies (each requiring its own separate application) or grant streams, this is essentially the most an individual can get from the Canadian government for creating any lone piece of work. And many grants either let you apply once a year or won't approve another grant until your previous project is confirmed completed, so concurrent funding is hard to pull off.

I wasn't bold enough to try to dip multiple pens in the government ink by pitching them every idea I might want to work on. Perhaps this is part of a personal failing that is holding me back from being more successful, but as my partially finished basement office will attest, I'm not really capable of doing more than one massive, self-directed project at a time. Theoretically I could try to cut down my turnaround time, or get better at winning multiple grants, but until such time as I figure those out, for me, $60,000 every two to three years is as much support as I can feasibly hope for.

Though, as I said, $25,000 was what I got. Between initial research, grant application, actual research, writing, and rewriting, this book took me a little over two meaningful (though not, as we'll get into, uninterrupted) years of work to complete. Even if I did it all in the thirteen months I foolishly promised I would do it in, the roughly $25,000 I got would still not count as a livable, let alone minimum, wage for my labour (at least in Canadian terms; even with the exchange rate, I'm beating the American rate by a cool $2). Not only did I not meet that timeline, I have a wife and two children who I'm fairly committed to not actively starving; astute readers will have noted that even with the maximum amount of money I can get from the national program explicitly designed to support the creation of artistic work in Canada, I presumably needed some other money to make this work.

Let's see if some radical, memoirish honesty is enough to earn me my artist badge here. I won't paste in the budget spreadsheet I fret over monthly, but for the time I spent writing this book, my family decided we needed a little under $8,000 a month, after taxes, to set our table. This puts us pretty much dead on the average household family in Alberta, where we live, although a cool $13,000 above the median per year. My instinct, having grown up underneath that mark, is to start sputtering off mealy-mouthed justifications about how thoroughly unworthy I am for any sympathy or financial support, but I'll admit to being someone with a healthy sense of self-worth/artistic ego and say a roughly average income doesn't seem like an unreasonable expectation for, well, any job at all, frankly. But definitely not one as culturally white-collar-coded as a writer. And extra-definitely not for me!

Setting aside my twitchy class nerves, I would say that this amount amounts to a certain serene security: almost all of my stresses are related to choices, not necessities; priorities, not paucity. I am able to indulge these impulses toward art or ego-stroking or windy philosophizing precisely because I am confident enough that, even if I have spent two years shitting the bed, I will be able to clean up my own mess. I hope it's not a failure of empathy – or artistic imagination – to say that I do not know how someone who doesn't have that particular bungee cord could just leap out into the void. Boldness cuts a romantic figure and all, but if hunger was the best motivator we'd be cutting funding to cancer researchers. If you love something, let it be comfortable enough to eat and think and imagine.

Much as I love to indulge my feelings and justifications on the matter, they're ultimately pretty much moot: my wife is doing all the heavy lifting here. Since I started writing books, she has contributed somewhere between 60 and 70 percent of our income, depending on precisely who wants to give me money for my little words in any given month. If her stated justifications for why she accepts this arrangement are to be believed, I owe this largesse to a mutual embrace of the tenets of feminist division of household labour ideas, and to the fact she thinks I'm a special little guy. I also have her family to thank for a down payment on a house, which I can say from experience unlocks a whole lot of tolerance, understanding, and interrelational progressivism, in addition to the more obvious financial security.

My wife is an even more profound benefactor when you consider that her earned money and family money granted me the other major source of my income, such as it was, during this whole book project: savings. I spent about eighteen months before the grant was deposited conceiving of this book, budgeting for the probable time it would take me to create it, applying for various grants, and waiting for news about whether I would actually get those grants, during which I was able to squirrel away about an extra $6,000 to supplement my grant. And I was only able to raise this amount because I spent the majority of this time doing advertising work for a freelance wage exorbitantly higher than anything I could ever dream of charging for the journalism, criticism, and essays. With the $5,000 I pulled aside from the sale of our previous house, I was almost set up to cover my monthly $3,000 contribution to the family finances for a year or so of writing. Added to the half of the $5,500 advance I got for signing the contract for this book, eighteen months' worth of freelance gigs that amount to another $4,000, $104 worth of royalty from my previous book, $100 I found outside the library while researching this book, and steady but unrelated payments from the Canada Child Benefit and Carbon Rebate programs, I was able to piece together enough of a buffer to allow for fourteen months of time focused mostly on putting this book together. When it became obvious that that wasn't going to cut it, I got various other jobs, which only served to slow things down further. In fairness to the grant program, that's on me.

What the grant was, then, was necessary but not sufficient. And maybe it's not even fair for me to call it necessary: I had savings, and support, and skills that allowed me a flexible enough day-ish job. Perhaps I could have pieced those things together and shown more steel between the doing-this-because-I-gotta-eat work, and the raising of children and attempting to be a decent partner to the person who supports me, and the helping of in-laws and parents who have also supported me, and the trying-to-carve-out-a-sense-of-self time.

But if some of the point of trying to be an artist is to know thyself, I can say I could not have done this without a grant. I need a constant source of external validation, which a jury of your peers represents. I am constitutionally incapable of devoting meaningful brain power to more than two important things in a day, and most days it's all I can do to give it to one. But most importantly, these things require time, and whatever my advantages, I need to buy it back from the world's demands in bulk. I had sort of hoped that by this point I would have written my own cheque for that purpose, but here we are. In every future I am comfortable picturing, I will be applying for these things until I'm dead – creatively if not literally.

Where I land with my personal grant is roughly where grants exist altogether: necessary but not sufficient. Unlike more personal forms of patronage, grants emerged as an ancillary to a much more important force defining art: the market. Whatever our thoughts on the importance of cultural meaning or the inherent worth of artistic pursuit, by the time grants came into being, both concepts were subservient to the idea that, if it's worthwhile, people will pay you for it without any intermediary. Until a more fundamental societal shakeup, grants are only ever going to be a consolation, another recognition that you get to call yourself an artist but not necessarily feed yourself off that fact.

4: There's a Kind of Unjustified Faith Involved Here
Beating the Market

Professional art is a contradiction in terms. Art is genius, and genius cannot belong to a profession. – William Hazlitt

It's hard to know things are ending until they have. So it's mostly inadvertent that David Byrne's 2012 book *How Music Works* now feels like it's documenting a bygone era. A mix of professional autobiography and wide-ranging theory on music and performance, it's a tour of a type of career that now feels increasingly impossible – especially for someone who subsumes commercial instincts to artistic exploration.

Two major music industry changes conspire to give *How Music Works* its archaeologic feel. In 2010, the ticket-selling platform Ticketmaster and the artist and event management company LiveNation completed a merger that would eventually give them control of over 70 percent of the concert market in North America, heavily weighted toward the most lucrative acts and shows. Then, in 2011, the music-streaming platform Spotify made its debut in North America, rapidly becoming the dominant player in what would become the near-exclusive way most people access and, in the loosest sense of the term, pay for music. These two developments would serve to push even harder on a lever that was already tilting away from artists: trusting the market to give artists a living.

It's worth lingering on this point. The de facto promise of market support of the arts has always been a screwy sort of promise, one of the earliest instances of what would become the neo-liberal ethos: it will create so much more money that, even if you're being treated unfairly – even if you are being massively exploited, in fact – you will end up better off than you would have been before. Or, at least, a few of you will. It's not quite winner takes all, but most of us will be left slurping at whatever spills over from the winners' bowls, mainly in the form of whatever other industry is created to keep things funnelling up.

Ticketmaster, in its pre-merger configuration, was as good an example of this as any. Founded in 1976, its original intent was to make the hardware and software necessary to run computerized ticketing systems. It was the only company using connected databases to develop a more efficient way to sell tickets – previously, concerts, even at stadium levels, would have relied on a single, central box office, or maybe passing out bundles to choice outlets, with no particularly good way of tracking who still had some left – and rapidly became the best at it, less through technological innovation than good old-fashioned market psychology. It began striking exclusive deals with major concert promoters and venues, offering chunky percentages and even multimillion-dollar advances paid for by its real innovation: service charges to the ticket buyer, which per the terms of agreement Ticketmaster was free to set at whatever it felt like.

This led to such rapid expansion that Ticketmaster was able to dictate terms to more or less anyone who wanted to put on a touring show in a large or concert-specific venue. In 1994, it famously torpedoed Pearl Jam shows – reneging on agreements to lower fees, disabling sales, and even threatening venues or promoters who tried to work with what was then one of the most popular bands in the world – because Eddie

Vedder had the temerity to complain about service fees and then try to stage a tour that didn't involve Ticketmaster at all. The tour was eventually cancelled, and Vedder tried to get the government to launch an anti-trust suit against the company, which ended up going nowhere.

Though most artists have learned their lesson about publicly complaining, these practices have gone into hyperdrive since the merger with LiveNation, which began by owning or controlling the booking at venues across the country and had recently begun signing artists to management deals outright: in 2007 and 2008, it signed Nickelback ($70 million), Shakira ($100 million), Madonna ($120 million), and Jay-Z ($150 million) to 360 deals that gave it a piece of every aspect of their business (recording, touring, merch, branded perfume, whatever). The combined company has since largely given up on management, in a bit of a why-buy-the-cow arrangement: between running tickets or outright owning venues, it controls access to the vast majority of places an artist who is even just beginning to get wider recognition would need to play in to make touring financially viable, so it can get its cut without paying upfront – and add on any other terms necessary to rack up the $22.75 billion in profit it made in 2023 (the pandemic was leaner, but that's still almost exactly double the company's 2019 margins).

Artists of a certain ilk can get a piece of this – Taylor Swift made headlines for making 1/22.75th of that on her Eras Tour. But unless you have enough cultural jam to strike a reasonable deal (and/or play multiple stadium shows per city), the restrictive terms and types of venues you have to play to avoid LiveNation are a big reason why most touring bands – even those that win awards, wind up on year-end lists, and sell out non-arena headlining tours – end their travels without enough to live on, if not with red ink. Canadian rapper Cadence Weapon documented how he lost over $2,000 on a one-month tour that followed up his 2021 win of the Polaris Prize, Canada's most prestigious album award, despite getting a $7,000 government grant to help offset costs.

———————

The post-pandemicness of it all has not helped, but touring was never a money-making prospect for most bands. In *How Music Works*, Byrne takes it as a given that tours are a promotional outlet, aiming for something around break-even to help goose album sales. Or they were when album sales were making artists money. That's increasingly not the case, thanks to Spotify and its streaming ilk.

Spotify was founded in 2006 and launched in its native Sweden in 2008, steadily expanding in the years that followed. It was trying to make access to music more efficient: buoyed by concerns about piracy that had followed digitization and higher-speed internet access, Spotify argued that it could erase the threat of piracy by offering a cheap (or even free, if you didn't mind ads and a lack of control) subscription to almost any song a listener could want. If stopping piracy losses is your only criterion, streaming has been a qualified success: according to the Recording Industry Association of America, in constant 2023 dollars, revenues from recorded music were about $17.1 billion in 2023 – down from the 1999 peak of $26.7 billion, but up from the nadir of $8.6 billion in 2014, and roughly in line with the 1970s heyday, if you disregard the U.S. population's having increased by about 50 percent since then.

The problem stems from the nature of how this money is distributed. Album sales in any format – cassette, LP, even digital download – typically guaranteed about a 10 percent royalty to the artist, with a bit more if the artist wrote all the music themselves (a 'mechanical royalty,' giving the company permission to mechanically reproduce the music, i.e., make a bunch more physical albums out of the masters). If we wanted to argue that online streams aren't quite the same thing as buying an album – say, it's more like playing the song on the radio – we're on even shakier ground. In the U.S., radio rates are typically determined through a complicated formula that involves stations of particular sizes paying flat fees that then get divided among songwriters based on how often the songs they've written are played. The U.S. is the only country that does it this way: most others pay royalties to both the writer and the performer. This number ends up varying wildly due to factors like the size and nature of the radio station, the total number of plays across the country (hit songs get bonuses), and other factors, but it is at least a couple bucks per play for commercial radio and can go as high as $20-plus in major markets; it's at least six cents per minute on college radio.

There have long been complaints about the relative fairness of those models. If they are working with any sort of record company, the people actually writing and performing the music never get the majority of the money generated by the recordings, and usually they get much, much less (again, 10 percent is industry standard). But even by those standards, streaming is an exceptionally bad deal. In 2023, Spotify claimed it distributed 50 percent ($4.5 billion of $9 billion) it made from subscribers and advertisers to record companies, to account for royalties. Half doesn't seem too bad, but back when everything was physical, retailers typically took only about 30 percent. Digital downloads were about the same, and even that was seen as a little egregious, since the distributors didn't have to pay for the infrastructure physical retailers did (rent, staff, etc.). Spotify also recently announced it's going to stop splitting any profits whatsoever with people whose songs have under one thousand streams. I mean, they weren't giving back a lot of money in the first place, but people don't usually announce in a press release that they are going to steal shit.

How Music Works was written in the early days of Spotify, but Byrne had experienced enough of it to know it wasn't designed to work for him. He attributes his lifetime earnings on the platform – $490 at the time – to his old band, which had managed a few million streams. It's certainly nice to earn a bit of money for a song you created thirty years ago, but at the standard record royalty, clearing that amount would have taken fewer than four hundred people – rather than a few million – paying for an album. I'll submit that at least four hundred people every year would have likely discovered a sudden need to buy a Talking Heads album if the entire catalogue wasn't available for about the same price per month.

It gets worse, although the worseness is not strictly Spotify's fault, insomuch as record companies are also using Spotify as a convenient opportunity to foist even worse deals on artists. Record companies have owned a chunk of Spotify since the beginning: when it launched, Sony, Universal, Warner, EMI (subsequently bought by Universal), and Merlin, a digital distributor for independent labels, owned a collective 20 percent. Now Sony and Universal hold on to about 7 percent between them, and the rest have divested. If apportioning blame is even messier than calculating radio royalties, what's very clear is how little the deal helps artists. Following an argument that song streams aren't sales but also aren't licensing, companies typically get away with sharing as little as possible of their Spotify money with artists: between about $0.003 and $0.005 per stream, according to industry estimates.

That can work out fine if you're the Weeknd, as of late 2024 the record holder for streams for a song, with 4.199 billion for 'Blinding Lights.' Assuming no other specific deal was struck, that's about $12 to $20 million on that song alone. An equivalent amount of radio play would have given him Jeff Bezos's ex-wife–level money, though obviously that'd be pretty much physically impossible. To get an equivalent payday at the usual album royalties, he'd have had to sell only about 10 million $20 copies – not a small number, but not even in the top 100 of all-time album sales, and about what the most popular album of each year did before digital distribution, legal and otherwise, became a factor.

And that's the most popular song, by about 350 million streams. By Spotify's own numbers, less than 2.3 percent of the 8 million artists with songs on the platform make $1,000 a year. About 0.2 percent make $50,000, which seems like a reasonable cut-off for calling music your main job, and we assume it doesn't cost you much of anything to record these songs (home recording set-ups are pretty good these days, even at mere disposable-income levels). Given that streaming of one kind or another makes up 75 to 80 percent of all recorded music money at this point, it seems fair to say that the 0.2 percent clearing fifty grand is a decent proxy for the number of current artists who can expect to earn a living just through recording music, if we leave out the number of people in that percentage who are dead.

If this is dire – and the fact that any musician below super-star level has almost no way to make money off recording seems pretty dire – it is only an evolution. The market has always been set up to reward an increasingly small percentage of actual artists. It is tremendously good at creating industries of people who make their money off artists, but just because the market will make money, and needs artists to make that money, doesn't mean artists will make money. If anything, technological innovation has only got more efficient at taking money even further away from artists.

If Spotify co-founder and CEO Daniel Ek's 2023 salary of $345 million were a song, it would need over 115 billion streams to earn him that much. The all-time leading streaming artist worldwide, Taylor Swift, managed 101.4 billion over the entire lifetime of Spotify up to early 2025. But, of course, Daniel Ek would never bother to write a song; he figured out how to make $345 million off other people writing songs. He didn't invent not paying them for it, but you don't make $345 million in one year by paying other people fairly. If anything, he's lucky that so much groundwork has been laid for making money off someone else's creative vision and ability.

––––––––––

As you did not find out about this book from a tasteful spread in *Architectural Digest* showing off my gorgeous built-in-shelved home office, you have probably surmised that I am not one of the grand winners of this particular game. But neither am I one of the more horrifically exploited (you have to achieve a higher level of success before you can be truly fucked over). What I am is one of the mushy middle for whom a basic, accepted-with-minimal-complaint level of exploitation is necessary to make the whole thing go. The system works as well for me as for anyone outside the tippity-top few percent, and the degree to which someone in my position might be inclined to complain corresponds to how comfortable they are keeping a machine going as long as it doesn't mangle them.

In a market system, me and artists like me are the public face of an industry that provides for a sizable if not vast number of people who aren't us to keep going. Some of these people are vital enough to this process that they could be considered artists in their own right but, in exchange for this lack of cultural prestige, tend to get rewarded with marginally steadier gigs and virtually no blame when things go wrong. In my world this is my editor; in other disciplines this ranges from curators to costumers to stagehands and roadies. (It's reasonably rare for someone to have only one of those jobs – I also edit books from time to time – but when you're doing this sort of thing, whatever salary you draw is most directly attributable to the creative work of somebody else.)

And beyond layers of maybe-artistic value, there are those of undeniable industry import: agents and publicists and managers and promoters and factory workers who manufacture books or records and the increasingly few people who work at the stores that sell them and ticket takers and art hangers and the people who clean the gallery after the launch party and CEOs and executive directors and so on. If it's easy to feel a certain way about other people taking 90-plus percent of what your work makes, thinking about (some of) these people softens things a bit. Some of them are directly helping your own art. And at least they're not working in tech or health insurance or something.

———————

This system turns artists not only into the front organization but also into a particularly mouthy kind of poker chip. Every artist who hands themself over to a cultural industry is being bet on, and as with all gambling, it is not the times you break even that keep you pushing your chips forward. I am allowed to do what I do because a very few of us win so big that the rest of us amount to a rounding error.

So, again, I'm a successful author, which means that as long as I can create books that do not lose money, the industry will probably keep letting me do it. Well, actually, I'm in a success superposition where if this one doesn't sell I'm no longer an author, I bet. (In the interest of full disclosure, I will say my editor made this note: 'Totally not true! We publish books by writers whose earlier books have TANKED all the time!!' Which is heartening, but I'll also note that she didn't say they'd publish *my* next book if *this one* TANKS.) My first book, *On Nostalgia*, was published in 2020. In its first year, it sold 1,400 copies; according to BookScan, that's better than at least 66 percent of authors do, especially during the pandemic. At the same time, I was in the 98 percent of books that did not sell more than 5,000 copies in the United States in 2020. I made a $2,500 advance on my first book, which was not paid off by the first year's sales. It took me two years to earn any royalty; as of 2025, I have made $2,982.37 total from that book. The drop-off in sales numbers is tightly correlated to the drop in pay, for good – or at least explicable – reason: almost all of the revenue that keeps publishers in business comes from either the top 10 percent of new books or the backlist (that is to say, not-new books). Backlist typically makes up about 70 to 80 percent of overall sales, so that's a very thin slice of a thin slice to be dividing for all those new books that don't immediately burst out of the gate or start making it up on the back end. And usually a book has to burst out of the gate to have a chance at even making, let alone selling on, the backlist; much of the money subsidizing the rest of us exists because those books keep selling well after they are made. Nothing is better for a balance sheet than a line item with substantially lower expenses.

These economics are vital to the industry, and in that sense vital for me, while at the same time not really doing a lot for me in real terms. It's been five years since *On Nostalgia* was published and started racking up that $2,982.37 in earnings. Even if I were more prolific, that is not going to pay for anything. Unless my books earn quite a bit more, quite a bit quicker, the free market is going to tolerate them but not go out of its way to make sure I can write them; that will be reserved for the people who have proven they can pick up the slack of people like me.

Now, I wouldn't be writing this if I wasn't convinced there was some chance to make an adequate living at it. I remember talking to a muralist friend who had done some work for Facebook in Toronto. Neither of us were particularly fans of the company, but that gig paid enough to let her keep doing whatever struck her artistically, from murals to art subscription services and paper crafts. We agreed that when we were younger and imagined selling out, it was for a mansion by the sea, not for the right to live in a two-bedroom apartment and call yourself a writer (or artist, in her case). But in my teens I gave up on being a lottery winner of any kind. I'm not going to turn down any windfalls, but my genuine dream at this point is just to be able to do this for the rest of my life.

———————

It is easy for me to look at a more distant past and imagine that it would have been a little bit easier to have been an artist then. There's no particular reason to believe it's gotten better, but it has never been, strictly speaking, good for artists. Good for *an* artist, if you're the right one – and, of course, everyone doing it believes they are. But it still feels like in another time I could have simply made sure I didn't cost anyone any money and found a way to make that into a living wage. Now, it seems, I have to have at least the potential to make someone else a lot of money to get any kind of real material comfort. Material comfort isn't why I do anything, but it does make it easier to do everything. (And if I was one of the market drivers, I would get to say things like 'The real honour is being able to subsidize all the wonderful literature coming out on this press,' cementing my status as the humblest author to ever sell five thousand copies in Canada.)

On the bright side, my relative lack of financial support is honest: no one has actively tried to fuck me over, it's just a consequence of the system. I swear I'm not trying to sound snidely ungrateful here: people trying to fuck you over is also, in its way, a consequence of the system, in that it's been happening for as long as we relied on the wider public for money.

————

My home industry of publishing may have had a slight head start at turning artists into a range of lucrative payoffs, but the form that has really excelled at using creative expression as seed capital is music. Some external factors are at play: songs are relatively short and we have a culture of playing them in the background of everyday life and even while we take in other works of art; we can consume, if not fully appreciate, music at rates that no other medium can touch. But that is at least partially because the industry can exploit the work of even a solitary individual in such a variety of ways. If we're going to return to our betting analogy, nothing else in the casino pays out like a popular musician.

It was a long and winding road to this particular door. For most of history, musicians were held back from really making money for themselves or others by their annoying need to be physically present for the performance. They took a step out of these brutal dark ages in 1548, when King Henry II of France granted the first publishing rights for books of music to Nicolas du Chemin, who may have been a musician but definitely owned a publishing house. What we now call musical notation is not much younger than regular old writing: samples from around 1200 to 1000 BCE have been found in Babylonia and India, and relatively independent systems cropped up through the next two thousand years in China, Japan, India again, Greece, the Byzantine Empire, and eventually Western Europe, which began the lineage of notation that's now considered standard. There's no evidence of a commercial motive until 1548: notation's original use was purely to share music – as Isidore of Seville, a music theorist writing in a place that didn't yet have a working notation system, put it, 'Unless sounds are held by the memory of man, they perish, because they cannot be written down.' He was only able to be a music theorist because he was also a monk, and it was attempts to share various hymns and chants and other assorted religious rituals that inspired quite a few of these notation systems.

In Europe, ecclesiastical notation was soon followed by tablature for organ and lute. Even though the latter was mostly played by troubadours and minstrels, who were absolutely looking to get paid for their troubles, there's no evidence anyone ever found a lucrative trade in copying these things out by hand and selling them – it was probably just easier to play the instrument and let people hear it. Things started to change with printing; it started with the Bible, obviously, but the second book ever printed was the *Mainz Psalter*, a book of psalms that included music to sing them by. It's so ingrained these days it hardly even seems like an idea someone would have to come up with, but it took about one hundred years for the problem of 'How exactly do you own a sound, let alone the representation of a sound, anyway?' to become a big enough deal that a king needed to weigh in on it. The licence Henry II extended tried to solve this problem by controlling who could print music, but it didn't take long for more licences to be extended (in more places, too), and for the idea of copyright (again, just a blindingly obvious term whose literal meaning gets lost in modern widespread usage) to pop up.

Music publishing was obviously lucrative enough for publishers to bother with – and for some people to pretend to be notable composers for a quick sale – but for the next few hundred years it was the equivalent of film novelization or published plays: you're not going to turn down the cheque, but that's not really why anyone's here. The actual money was in court composing and concert halls until about the mid-nineteenth century, when it became fashionable for middle-class families to have pianos in their living rooms. These instruments weren't just there to hold the family's photos and dashed dreams – they were entertainment machines; playing for and with the family and visitors was the entire point. Sheet music was more essential to the enjoy-ment than tuning. The growing industry found its way into entertainment outside the home, too, providing the sound-tracks for cabarets, minstrel shows, cafés, and saloons.

For the major names you're thinking of when I say 'nine-teenth-century music,' the sheet music industry was not a major concern; the real boon was for people who were never going to play in courts, operas, or concert halls. It was now lucrative to sell music without ever playing it in front of people. (It also created new performing work: 'song pluggers' were employed by music stores to demonstrate new sheet music for customers, providing early jobs for the likes of George Gershwin and Irving Berlin.)

Stephen Foster, writer of 'Oh! Susanna,' 'Camptown Races,' and the twenty-million-sheet-music-selling 'Old Folks at Home,' sometimes called the first American composer, was entirely self-taught and spent more time in public drink-ing and chasing women than performing. He began publish-ing music while he was in high school and found a lucrative career in writing minstrel songs – though he was white, he claimed his ambition was to be 'the best Ethiopian songwriter,' which was indeed a euphemism for the word you're thinking of – while he was working at a cotton mill in Cincinnati. His unwillingness or inability to play concerts for money contrib-uted to his dying a destitute alcoholic in 1864, although what most contributed to his destitution was his decision to sell his entire existing and future output to his publishing company, Firth, Pond & Co., for $1,900, to help pay for his growing drinking habit. (More like America's first rock star, am I right.)

Things worked out a little better for 'I Love You Truly' writer Carrie Jacobs-Bond, probably the bestselling sheet music writer/composer of the nineteenth century, and only slightly more of a performer than Foster. A musical prodigy, she almost never performed outside of people's houses, even though one of those performances was at the White House. Jacobs-Bond was a homemaker and piano teacher who began writing songs at the behest of her husband, who noticed she always seemed to be singing them; she began living off them after he died from slipping on some ice. She made the wise financial choice to start her own publishing company (she even did the artwork for most of her covers), although it was as much out of necessity as shrewdness; most publishing companies wouldn't have anything to do with a woman. The Carrie Jacobs-Bond & Son publishing company helped her keep almost all the money made off her music, letting her retire in Hollywood (again, the template for American musical success was set some time ago).

Jacobs-Bond's career spanned the next great innovation in making a lot of money off music: recording. If mere sheet music couldn't rewire a musician's priorities, recording definitively shifted the money seesaw from performing it in front of people to creating it and letting mechanical reproduction handle the rest. Almost as quickly, it shifted the flow of money from the person who created the music to the person who controlled the means of production. As music historian Michael Chanan explains in his book *Repeated Takes: A Short History of Recording and Its Effects on Music*, it was virtually as soon as the phonograph began appearing in homes that 'musicians began to experience recording as a new and contradictory form of exploitation, in which other people were always making more from records than they did,' with the caveat that 'the rewards to be gained with success often outstripped all other sources of musical money-making.' Which is how you get people signed on to a system they can recognize as notably exploitative: give them enough money that they don't care, which usually just translates as 'more money than they can get for doing it some other way.' Or at least the promise of more money.

If musicians had another reason to feel suspicious, it's because recording has always been a business. Unlike sheet music, it did not evolve out of singing God's praises; it evolved out of selling gramophones. The first recording devices were supposed to be an improvement on the secretary, capturing the notes and thoughts of businessmen. It was only as recording quality and playback length improved that it occurred to some phonograph companies that people might want to listen to something other than their boss.

The Columbia Phonograph Company – technically the oldest surviving recording company, though equally as technically a brand name that has been passed around by parent companies for about a century (since 1988, it has been a division of Sony) – started in 1889 with nothing but an exclusive licence to sell Edison phonographs and phonographic cylinders in the District of Columbia. This was a lucrative market, what with all the people who wanted to record themselves speaking. Within fifteen years, they had graduated to a very rudimentary version of what we now think of when we say 'a record' (a pressed disc format) and started recording Metropolitan Opera singers, like most of their rivals did. One of the earliest proofs of concept for the notion that pairing with recording companies could work out okay for a performer came from opera singer Enrico Caruso, who signed with rival company Victor; he earned a $4,000 flat fee plus a 30 to 40 percent royalty, making him about $6 million in his sixteen-year recording career. Though he still got less than half of what was made off the thing he created, it was a nearly unprecedented position to be in, then or now; unless you were famous enough to demand royalties, most musicians just got a flat fee for playing on the record. America's 1909 Copyright Act guaranteed the writers of music, as well as the publishers, a royalty from its being recorded and played. In this case, being forced to share with at least one of the artists worked out rather well for the record companies, attracting talent and helping recorded music overtake sheet music as people's preferred way of buying songs, growing the money pool for everyone involved. This gradually helped to give the performers more power and more ability to force their way into higher paydays – though that was by no means guaranteed.

This overall trajectory isn't that different from, say, an app gradually becoming one of the top producers of filmed content. To the degree Columbia Records is like YouTube, they both started out selling platforms and quickly realized it was very helpful to also make content that the platform could use. The platform didn't create the artists, but it gave them another aspect to experiment with, a tool with which to reshape their art and the new platform; Columbia Records did not exactly give the world Louis Armstrong, Frank Sinatra, Johnny Cash, Bob Dylan, and Beyoncé, but recorded music did, and recorded music is entirely a creature of the business that created it.

———

No new artistic opportunity has ever created a fairer world, especially not if it was made to be a business. This legacy is written across a century of almost fully documented lives and recordings, but we can sum up a pretty good chunk of it with the song 'Hound Dog.' It was created under circumstances that were convoluted, though not unique. In 1952, Johnny Otis was hired by then-Peacock record company head Don Robey to do something with a singer Peacock had signed. Big Mama Thornton had been singing with travelling shows since she was fourteen years old, after winning a talent contest; Robey signed her ten years later, when she started singing at his Bronze Peacock Club in Houston. Her first album did okay in Houston but failed to gain attention nationally; she took a side job shining shoes while Robey struck a deal with Otis, a touring bandleader who had a habit of 'discovering' stars, which usually meant a combination of giving them a steady gig and finding them songs to perform. Otis brought in songwriters Jerry Leiber and Mike Stoller to write something specifically for Thornton, and some combination of the four of them (they would fight about the exact responsibilities for decades afterward) produced 'Hound Dog.' Its story – of a woman chasing out a useless man trying to use her – was sold by Thornton's ferocious, knowing performance; the recording spent seven weeks at the top of the sales charts, moving some 500,000 copies, and solidified if not outright launched the national careers of everyone involved.

Owing to a quirk of the 1909 Copyright Law that helped solidify if not outright launch the record industry, covers, interpretations, and thematic responses to 'Hound Dog' popped up almost immediately; until the updated law in 1976, once a recording had been produced, anyone was free to create their own recording of that particular song, so long as they informed the original copyright holders of their intention to do so. 'Hound Dog' had ten of these within three years, although the only one that would really matter in the long run was by Freddie Bell and the Bellboys, the house band for Las Vegas's Sands Casino. With simplified lyrics that lost a lot of the innuendo and fury of the original, this was the version that caught Elvis Presley's ear in April 1956, and he began using it as the closing number in his live shows. A few months later, his halting, exaggerated dance to it on *The Milton Berle Show* saw him condemned across the country as gutter trash. He recorded the song one month after that and released it as a B-side with 'Don't Be Cruel'; they would become his second and third number-one hits, selling over 5 million copies.

I assume I do not have to tell you what became of Elvis. Leiber and Stoller were credited as the songwriters on Presley's version as well, which set them up for life, though they would also go on to write plenty of other hits, including 'Jailhouse Rock,' 'Stand by Me,' and their most important work, 'Yakety Yak.' Johnny Otis parlayed 'Hound Dog''s success into a life-long career, including eponymous TV and radio shows, and possibly the most critically lauded travelling R&B revue to ever exist. Don Robey used the success of 'Hound Dog' to merge with Duke Records, establishing the most successful Black record label in the country until Berry Gordy's Motown came along about a decade later; he sold his label to Lou Adler in 1973 and died of a heart attack two years later.

Big Mama Thornton made $500 off her song, which sold 500,000 singles. She was never properly credited for its creation, copyright-wise, in her lifetime. Its popularity did keep her in gigs and on the Peacock Records roster for most of the 1950s, but she eventually moved to San Francisco in the 1960s, hoping it would offer more opportunity than Houston. She apparently did not think much of the city's musicians, but she kept performing and recording and managed to secure some of the royalties when Janis Joplin decided to record Thornton's song 'Ball and Chain' for Big Brother and the Holding Company's album *Cheap Thrills*. The fresh attention, and cash flow, allowed Thornton to tour Europe and North America in connection with various jazz and blues festivals and revues for the rest of her life, although she was increasingly hampered by heavy drinking. She last performed in 1983 and died penniless in a rooming house in 1984, though her funeral was attended by Otis and many other of her friends in the music business. She was also inducted into the Rock & Roll Hall of Fame in 2024, for what that is worth.

Peter Lewis, who played guitar on 'Hound Dog' and who Leiber and Stoller credited with writing the riff that inspired the song, received a day rate for his work on the recording. He played in Otis's band until 1956, when he was kicked out, and is said to have made a living playing L.A. nightclubs until at least the mid-sixties. It's believed he died, homeless, in about 1970.

———

The plight of musicians over the last century and a half is not much different than that of any worker thrown into an open market: the surplus of labour and concentration of capital will always make their position precarious and allow for exploitation. The solution most workers settle on is the union – historically, anyway. Unions aren't what they used to be, but around the time Big Mama Thornton was recording 'Hound Dog,' they were at the height of their power, with a full third of the labour force active union members. The fact that no one involved in the creation of that particular song had a union card, and that union membership among most musicians (and other artists) today is relatively rare, is a function of the unique challenges of organizing creative workers and also of some happenstance historical quirks.

We should qualify that one artistic pursuit is almost universally unionized: acting. And everything that involves acting in some capacity. From the biggest-budget films to the smallest regional professional theatres, almost everyone involved with the creation and production of North American film, television, and theatrical works – from A-listers to the people who put tape on the floor to mark cues, and every sound designer and costume mender in between – is a card-carrying union member. The simplest explanation for this is not that there is a higher rate of Marxists in the performing arts as much as that these sorts of pursuits have always required hiring significant groups of people to pull off, and groups are easier to both regulate and organize. A brief history of musicians' unions should show why that's such a key factor.

In North America, musicians' unions of some kind or another track relatively closely with other labour unions: collective organizations setting pay scales and regulating members popped up in various cities in the 1870s and first came together as the National League of Musicians in 1886. Less than a decade later, a breakaway group petitioned to get the American Federation of Labor to recognize the American Federation of Musicians, which is the organizing body for instrumental musicians to this day.

The reason for the split has a lot to do with perpetual issues that confront artists trying to organize. One of the biggest fault lines in the National League of Musicians was between more established musicians – many of whom made their entire living from performing or in some cases compos-ing music – and generally younger and more precarious musi-cians, who often had to work other jobs. It's a classic craft union vs. labour union debate, shot through with the ego of people whose particular skill has been celebrated as rarified. The established/craft forces operate more like a medieval guild, ensuring only sufficiently skilled practitioners are even able to call themselves professional musicians, setting prices for the purposes of ensuring these skilled people don't accidentally undercut each other, and providing things like pensions and insurance. The up-and-comer/labour side of things had many of the same concerns, but generally presented as more egalitarian: less concerned with credentials, they were happy to represent you as long as you were willing to do the work and (literally) pay your dues. Though the labour side ostensibly won out in the 1890s, this tension never really resolved itself, and a version of this debate is basically why pop music never managed to be unionized. (Well, that and the racial tensions that also never really resolved themselves, about which more in a second.)

For at least the first fifty years of its existence, the American Federation of Musicians (which also covers Canada) managed to subsume these tensions and present a mostly united front. For the first twenty-five years, this was partly because all of its members worked in what we'd now consider to be the classical music tradition, and recording and playback technology wasn't yet good enough to challenge the supremacy of live performance.

Both facts were challenged starting in the 1920s. Diminishing the dominance of classical music was the rise of ragtime and its successor, jazz. Owing to jazz's roots as Black music and its tendency to be performed outside the concert halls to which the unions dictated terms, its musicians were not hastily welcomed into the union. They might have remained permanently outside, like pop performers, were it not for a triple threat to all North American musicians: a cabaret tax that scooped up 20 percent of the profits of any venue where music was performed; Prohibition, which massively reduced the profitability of such venues; and the increasing viability of recorded music, which threatened to make a person playing in front of a crowd obsolete. Enough common ground was found for solidarity to win out – though the fundamental issues continued to fester.

Nowhere was this better demonstrated than in the recording strike of 1942–44. One of the most successful artistic labour actions in history, it inadvertently hastened the obsolescence of the Federation, at least as far as popular music was concerned. The strike was the culmination of almost twenty years of improving recording technology with no concordant improvement in the way musicians were treated by recording companies. The first blow, in the mid-1920s, was the invention of the 'talkie,' films that synced a recorded soundtrack with the moving image. By some estimates, this cost up to a quarter of working musicians in the United States their main gig: playing in the pit orchestra for movies. Decent recordings took over other areas musicians could rely on. Though the major concert halls were unaffected, radio stations began replacing in-house bands in the 1930s, and halls, bars, and other small venues turned to juke-boxes around the same time, giving them the double advantage of not needing to pay a musician and not needing to pay the cabaret tax.

Recordings were still paid like gigs, but they could be used indefinitely by the company that made them. By 1937, musicians in individual cities began demanding their union leaders do something, and five years later there was sufficient anger for the Federation to ignore the wartime ban on labour actions and shut down recording until the major record labels agreed to a royalty structure. With a backlog that helped float new sales for several months, the first company, Decca, didn't crack until a year in. The other two majors, Columbia and RCA, lasted another year after that, at least partly because they hit on a surprisingly lucrative loophole: vocal recordings.

Singers were largely left out of the union, at least partly because of the compromise that had been struck between the classical and jazz musicians when they came together: as long as you could sight-read a composition, you counted as a musician. Almost all of the musicians, even jazz improvisors, had some classical style of training. So did many vocalists attached to big bands, but they never had any cause to demonstrate it, and until the 1940s they were such a minor part of most performances, live or recorded, that unionizing them wasn't a pressing issue. So when the musicians refused to record, enterprising recording executives brought in up-and-comers like Frank Sinatra, Bing Crosby, and Perry Como, with backing tracks provided by vocal groups. By the time the musicians returned, these singers had become so popular they now regularly took top billing over band leaders. Of course, jazz musicians and big-name band leaders still made their own high-profile releases for decades afterward, but the bell could not be unrung.

The real body blow to the Federation came in the form of rock and roll. Sinatra and his fellow crooners still relied on union musicians for everything but their singing, and the royalty cheques the union had won stabilized, if not precisely rejuvenated, the profession. Rock and roll – and the genres that influenced and fed off it, like blues, rhythm and blues, and country – was a model that the Federation's existing framework couldn't account for. As Michael James Roberts explains in his history of the battles between rock and the union, *Tell Tchaikovsky the News: Rock 'n' Roll, the Labor Question, and the Musicians' Union, 1942–1968*, it came down to three essential features: the Federation's insistence on classical education (namely the ability to read music), the importance of recording to rock's aesthetic (rock musicians learned and primarily shared their music through recording, whereas the Federation favoured live performance above all), and rock's adoption of a countercultural attitude.

Perhaps needless to say, rock's roots in music created and popularized by largely uneducated Black musicians were an underlying factor in all of this. So was a snobbery about what constituted art. Rock was entertainment, and large swaths of union leadership and membership resisted it as a passing fad that did not measure up to their august traditions. (The Federation even fought against the Beatles' first American tour on the grounds that 'we can go to Yonkers or Tennessee and pick up four kids' capable of playing their songs.) The fact that most bands in this tradition were self-contained units who rarely needed to employ any other musicians to help them write, play, or record – they did need producers, but unlike many of their big-band counterparts, these bands were usually employing producers for help with songs they had written, not being contracted to record a song someone else had written – only made the dismissal mutual.

The Federation did eventually make room for rock-focused musicians, especially among session players: the famous Wrecking Crew, who helped make hits like 'Be My Baby,' 'Good Vibrations,' and 'Mrs. Robinson,' were all union members, although most of them were also classically trained. But by then the template had been set: by the time rock's groundwork gave way to evolutions like punk and hip-hop, so much infrastructure, from venues to recording methods, had nothing whatsoever to do with Federation norms that the union became almost exclusively the home of institutional musicians, the types who fill out orchestras and jazz ensembles at major halls and occasional recording studios. Most popular musicians are not even technically eligible for Federation membership, although they could apply; pop stars on major labels like Universal and Sony are technically represented by SAG-AFTRA, the film and television actors' union, although few of them bother to pursue membership. All of them do pretty directly benefit from the royalty structures that the Federation fought for in the 1940s, though. (Or did before streaming came along to blow that up.)

According to the stats, most of the working musicians in North America, some seventy thousand, are actually unionized; according to the charts, most of the music that people actually listen to is created by non-union musicians – many of whom are doing just fine but many, many more of whom are struggling mightily or might be, soon. As popular musicians start to face the same realities their classical brethren did eighty years ago, they might consider the same fix.

Whatever the future may hold, our popular conception of a musician is not of a union man. I'm not sure if David Byrne was born at the absolute ideal time to make money off music as an artist, but I do know his career would have been more or less impossible one generation earlier. It was maybe possible one generation later, but that seems to be the last generation, for now. The market will make money, and it will need artists, but that doesn't mean artists will make money. This isn't some pessimistic prediction: this is how markets have always worked, especially when artists are involved. Spotify and LiveNation are a new kind of manager, but we don't need new technology to rip off artists (although it definitely helps). That said, just because it's never been good doesn't mean someone somewhere hasn't had it best.

However bad the business model for Byrne, he did come along at a time when it became massively easier for any one person to speak to thousands, maybe millions, of people. From his first days as a busker in the late 1960s to directly selling an album to his fans on his website in 2008, he was present to experience unprecedented opportunities and see them being scooped up by someone who came to make money, not music.

A good number of those opportunities had nothing whatsoever to do with music, such as cheap rent in New York City (though that has been equally scooped up). But even if we limit ourselves to the business Byrne eventually found himself in, he had an uncanny knack for making the most out of things that paid. You can't be a busker for very long if you miss what the crowd is telling you; in the market, money is just another way to listen.

Byrne never started any clothing lines or anything, but financial as much as artistic success in his long era of making music has involved knowing how to manage at least some aspect of your business, whether that's image or investment or just good accounting. In *How Music Works*, he gives a pretty detailed accounting of his albums *Grown Backwards* and *Everything That Happens*, and he reveals himself to be a fastidious and efficient money manager – not the most expected qualities for someone whose most famous image is a comically oversized parody of a grey salaryman, but being careful about money is in its way as important an artistic gesture for Byrne's success as his ability to craft something like an iconic grey suit. You can't be an artist of Byrne's stature in Byrne's time without a sense of creativity and also of what kind of creativity people will buy.

This doesn't have to be read as nefarious. Byrne is simply responding to his audience, shaping his expressions so that they can be maximally understood. He understands money not as an end in itself but as a tool that allows him to pursue his impulses as much as is reasonable and that works as a stand-in for direct audience response. His track record – following up a landmark pop-rock album with ambient recording experiments, modern dance performances, directing a kitschy satirical musical, launching a world music label, and releasing another landmark album – suggests his core impulse is to find a way to say something about the world. But you don't get to have a career that varied unless you know how to make art that perfectly coheres to a budget that leaves you with enough to make more. Byrne has all the business savvy of a modern pop star brand; he simply chose Broadway musicals over perfume.

Outside of any particular wisdom or instinct on his part, though, it was a lucrative time to be making music, thanks to trends that began well before Byrne was even born. Take his most basic tools: instruments and recording equipment.

Instruments have been in houses for a long time, but industries devoted to selling instruments followed the middle-class piano boom. By Byrne's time, children were regularly given instruments as gifts – Byrne tells a story of playing a melodica as a four-year-old – and standardized, high-quality instruments were universally available, penetrating every conceivable demographic slice. Whether you played a violin or a fiddle, electric guitar or stand-up bass, said something about your strata, sure, but everyone had something. Slightly rarer was recording equipment: Byrne was recording to magnetic tapes when he was an eight-year-old. He obviously wasn't selling those tapes, but it does mean something – there are no extant recordings of Beethoven or Liszt or Wagner actually playing music, but the Talking Heads guy has stuff from grade school. The widespread adoption of magnetic tape as the preferred medium for recording music led directly to the most nakedly lucrative period for music (and, incidentally, some musicians) currently feasible. One day someone blew into a reed, and one day tens of thousands of years later somebody figured out that if you put the right frequencies on some magnetic tape you'll be able to make as many copies of that little tune as anyone will ever want. And they will give you money for those copies. You've already seen how much.

Luckily for Byrne, the full extent of that effect was still being sorted out when he began. Recording hadn't advanced so much that it was seriously competing with live performance. Even something as simple as busking makes slightly more sense when no one has headphones, but Byrne pretty quickly found gigs that weren't on street corners.

His first forays into performances people were specifically coming for was in coffee shops. A wave of Italian immigration had brought cafés that served espresso in a relaxed atmosphere. This, combined with a growing interest in discovering American folk music – some of which had been recorded and so could finally be heard outside of the place the folks lived – created a movement of open-minded cultural venues with enough customers to fill the occasional hat. Byrne didn't turn any heads on the coffee shop circuit, but his ambitions and attention evolved with the format. Mickey Ruskin, a lawyer who opened increasingly ironically named restaurants and clubs, began with the Tenth Street Coffee-house before opening Max's Kansas City, the proto-punk bar that set the template for the art-inclined drinking holes that would serve as the support system for Talking Heads and more or less every other 1970s New York guitar-based band you know of.

Max's and its spiritual successors CBGB, Mudd Clubb, Club 82, the Mercer Arts Center, and a dozen more were booking a few bands every night. Byrne and Talking Heads were able to play almost weekly, the hundredish bucks not quite enough to cover rent, even when you were sharing, but certainly enough to provide plenty of time and motivation to keep on playing. (Though it is worth underlining they were able to get reasonable rent on places large enough to double as rehearsal/studio spaces.) Venues centred on musicians weren't new, obviously, but because of their modest scale – most were small enough to avoid the taxes, dues, and civic fees required of more purpose-built music venues – and their quantity before recorded music became sufficient entertainment for the crowd they attracted, these spaces provided more opportunity for untrained bands than existed before or since.

If these proved to be Byrne's foundation, the edifice that really solidified things financially was coming up right behind. The first stadium show was the Beatles at Shea in 1965, but the general idea of arenas as venues would really perk up in the 1970s, as professional basketball and to a lesser extent hockey began to expand, building more stadiums for more money. These buildings needed something to play in them 320 nights of the week. Not a whole lot of musicians ever headline arenas, obviously, but arenas are the only place where millions of dollars enter the equation. By the time

Byrne perfected the art of playing arenas, those venues were more a sign of the millions than its source: touring, even at the arena scale, was still about advertising the album. A show that massive sucks up a lot of resources – and a lot of people make solidly middle-class livings helping set up, run, and support those shows – but the real money was in albums: recordings that could be printed, paid for, and played as often as anyone wanted.

It is not a coincidence that the bestselling Talking Heads albums are tightly tied to 1983's Remain in Light Tour, their first and last experience primarily playing arenas, coliseums, and civic centres (even if the landmark concert film *Stop Making Sense* was filmed in a converted and relatively modest three-thousand-seat movie theatre): *Remain in Light* cracked a million, while the *Stop Making Sense* live album and 1985's *Little Creatures*, which immediately followed it, topped 2 million units apiece. Even those numbers were not good enough to crack the Top 30 album sales in their release years, to give a sense of how many albums were being sold at the time.

At the standard roughly 10 percent royalty, that was enough to set Byrne up for life, not only from the initial windfall but from the real key to comfort for an artist of any kind: making money off your old work. Though Spotify would eventually cause most of that to dry up, even just one big Top 10 hit ('Burning Down the House') and a handful of albums that lived in the memories of boomers, who in turn passed the legend down to their children, were enough to keep a steady drip of radio play, reissues, and purchases by new discoverers rolling through the intervening decades, a lottery-like cushion from one brief period of his career that makes it a little easier to take some of those wild swings he liked (though he also famously prefers biking around to taking cars, so there's bound to be some savings to stretch there, too).

Then there are the spin-off benefits: achieving this level of popularity assured Byrne enough stature to keep him in adequate paydays for the rest of his life. He was also around when that aspect started to pay off in direct ways: part of his accounting in *How Music Works* shows how he made more money from self-releasing *Everything That Happens Will Happen Today* than he did from the conventionally released *Grown Backwards*. But he is also forthright about how that would have been essentially impossible if he was not, you know, David Byrne (*and* Brian Eno, in the former case); it's easier to play in a slightly democratized, direct-pay, attention economy if you have a few decades of industry-supported promotional attention to play off.

———————

Two things are worth saying explicitly here. The first is that it can be easy to slip into envious cynicism about any number of the broad forces that played a direct role in Byrne getting this sort of life: the favourably sloped playing field most boomers of his ilk enjoyed, happening to get in before the confluence of corporate powers belatedly but forcefully real- ized how to suck money further and further away from workers of all descriptions; the tendency of listeners to retreat to well-worn hits and artists from long ago instead of pushing themselves to search for their modern equivalents; et cetera et cetera. I hope I don't come off like that. I'm deeply jealous, of course, but I'd rather a world where everyone had those opportunities than one where everyone is left to fight it out in our brand of muck. Byrne deserves those opportunities as much as any singularly brilliant (or uniquely devoted) artistic voice does.

The second is that I have purposely avoided trying to talk much about Byrne's actual art here. This is only partly because I am checking my personal tendency to take a variety of stimulants and harangue someone about *Stop Making Sense* into the wee hours of the morning; it's also because I'm trying to limit him to a business, man. Now, it feels ugly to reduce Byrne, an artist whose work has rewired parts of my understanding of the world, to a savvy operator, even if I'm arguing that's part of his genius. I hope this comes across as a tribute to something that, as a financial possibility and as a specific mode of art, seems to be passing away. Byrne, of course, has plenty to say about the peculiar form of alienation any kind of capital brings to the human soul. I encourage you to go look some of it up, but at this particular moment I just want you to sit with the feeling of reducing art to a market strategy, because quite a few people do this every single day, some for quite a bit of money.

Because I'm not a complete dick, I should say that a great number of them love art just as much as I do, and got into the business because they were equally affected by it, and are doing their part to bring more of it into the world. That's money for you, though: think about it enough and it fills the space you made for other things.

5. I Wish I Did Not Have to Write the Instruction Manual
Is It a Side Gig If It's the Main Way Everyone Pays Their Bills?

I do not have the most extensive artistic resumé, but still, across my career, I have not once been able to fully devote myself to the creation of an artistic work for the entire time it took to create it. And I've certainly never had any fallow periods or breaks in between. Everything I have ever made – by my count, two non-fiction books, a self-published graphic novel, a good handful of creative non-fiction essays, and some mostly unpublished/unproduced fiction and screenplays – has come between other things, even if those other things were only part-time gigs. Some of them were reasonably creative in and of themselves, like journalism; a lot of them, like crafting encyclopedia articles or ad copy or event invitation emails, directly used my creative faculties; some were entirely unrelated, like pouring coffee or reading gas meters. But there has always been something.

I know enough other artists to know this is a common state of affairs, especially when the list of other things includes teaching people how to be artists. And it's not as if these other jobs are horrific compromises: I like most of the ones I've had, even those that aren't directly applicable to my artistic ambitions. I've done some purely mercenary things, absolutely, but by and large I've managed to get work that satisfies some other aspect of my being and pays reasonably well. I'm choosing between shades of desire and meaning, not between eking out a starving-artist living and cremating corpses.

Still, what bothers me, if I'm being honest, is that I don't see a world where that isn't always the case; the prospect of being a full-time artist without an admin or freelance job tugging at my time seems fully impossible, or such a lottery-level event that it's not worth seriously considering. Even if this is a natural state of things, it's hard not to feel I'm doing something wrong. Somewhere deep in the back of the mind, that part that emerges in the wee hours or particularly potent cases of writer's block, I am convinced that I can't really consider myself an artist because it's never going to fully cover my bills. It's never going to be the only thing. A lot of this worry is existential: if some significant part of the creative impulse is to figure out yourself, figure out the world, it blows a rather large hole in the project to admit that I can't even settle the 'Am I an artist?' question.

The rational part of me, which crafts outlines and engages in rigorous research and comes up with excuses for my editor, has plenty of justifications for calling myself whatever I like. I write, I make things, I am an artist. And people pay me for this! Private companies and public institutions! Individual people, even! Assuming that continues, I am on solid ground here.

But if there is no reasonable definition by which I'm not an artist, there's still a distressing unreasonable doubt that, well, no, I am not, I am just a hobbyist, and maybe even a delusional one at that. I'm not entirely without ego, but it's not that I feel I *deserve* a suitably comfortable living doing exactly what it is I want. I think it's something about my state being permanently irreconcilable: even if I were a full-time artist who eventually had to go back to day jobs, I would have had some answer. As it is, I am stuck in the realm of being able to make *something* at it without being able to make *enough* at it, which leaves plenty of room for doubt and confusion. Am I deluding myself? If I stop doing this, was everything that led up to it just a waste? Should I stop because then at least I would have an answer? But instead I keep on in this superposition of artistic legitimacy, perpetually not quite but never truly not.

This feeling only seems to get more potent as I age. I don't think that's because of impending mortality – at least that offers a resolution – so much as the rest of life increasingly impinging. When you're younger, you are supposed to spend time figuring things out, living with possibilities; you're supposed to do some of that when you're older, too, but meandering questions about who I really am feel like excessive indulgences now that I have a wife and two children. Maybe I'm just worried I'm sacrificing the little time I have with them on an altar to a dream I had when I was a teenager who used books and movies as a stand-in for a social life. Maybe I'm worried that unless one of these books provides a solid education (and a reasonable retirement for me, too), they will forever regard me as trading them for an empty promise. Or maybe I think I could do some incredible things if nothing else impinged on my days.

I've never quite been able to resolve it. What inevitably lets me put it to rest – besides inevitably abandoned promises to quit entirely – is the knowledge that I am not alone in this. By far the most common type of artist is the one who has to split their time, who finds some other way to support their creative aspirations. It's not enough to kill the doubts entirely, but given that we're all out here trying to make some kind of connection through our work, there's something beautiful in the notion that we're making a go of it however we can.

The idea of being an artist is in some sense the promise of freedom. Freedom is not all it is cracked up to be – a blank page is often a terrifying prospect, more so the longer it stays blank – but we are all indoctrinated in the cult of the individual, and being able to choose precisely who we are and what we do is theoretically some inborn right, although more practically it's something like our highest ideal. The artist is one of those figures who, in popular if not personal conception, is allowed – or maybe has taken, has earned – the ability to do whatever it is they want to do: put a crucifix in a jar of piss, discard the bounds of morality and taste, paint a gaudy moonlit cottage, turn petty grievances into illuminating truths about the human condition. It is about the only way a person can maintain standing in society while indulging their unfettered self, besides being rich.

Of course, it helps immensely to be a rich artist. Few artists of any standing have understood that better than George Gissing. He is not especially widely read today. Even by the standards of his Victorian counterparts, his sentences can be laborious, and his writing is shot through with a prosaic pessimism that is neither grandiose enough to suck in moody teens nor implicitly redeemed by some hard-won wonderment (his earliest biographer, Frank Swinnerton, described him as 'temperamentally unhappy'). Gissing does have enough regard for people – maybe more so men – to attempt to see them fully, frustrations, pettiness, and bitterness very much included, which is partly why he was regarded, along with Thomas Hardy, as one of the best late-Victorian novelists, and why Orwell was willing to call him, with caveats, among the best English novelists ever.

In Orwell's words, Gissing's overarching subject was 'a protest against the form of self-torture that goes by the name of respectability,' which is a sort of roundabout way of saying that Gissing mostly wrote, in brutal and blatantly (self-) pitying terms, about what it felt like to have less money than you thought you should. Not really concerned with the absolute poor, who he didn't despise so much as consider unworthy of thinking about in any direction, Gissing was a patron saint of the perpetually aggrieved who were close enough to understand how crucial money was to the project of respectability without ever really being able to get their hands on it. (Personally, Gissing's Gollum-y persecution complex would be easier to dismiss if it didn't feel like it was stabbed out of my spleen; it doesn't really make sense to get mad at the doctor who biopsies your cancer for showing you what ugly, horrible things live inside you.)

The real masterpiece of this horrifically accurate assessment of humanity is in his 1891 novel *New Grub Street*, named for the eighteenth-century den of Bohemians, hacks, and gutter rags that was, in Gissing's view, the model for contemporary publishing. It's a story of two writers: Edwin Reardon, a nominally talented novelist whose artistic sensibilities and mounting frustration with his resolutely middle-class prospects leave him unable to write, and Jasper Milvain, a cynical striver who is quite happy to write whatever pays. Milvain's convictions about financial stability extend so far that he is happy to hate his presumed public and totally unwilling to marry a woman he genuinely likes because he needs a richer wife to secure his future as a man of letters. If these two now feel like mythical archetypes, it may be less about the novel's direct influence than the universality of people's (especially artists'?) hatred of anyone who outdoes them, and their search for moralistic or spiritual explanations of their relative positions. (Money cannot help but be virtue for anyone who has it and will never be virtue for anyone who doesn't.)

The novel, if not directly autobiographical, is shot through with Gissing's own experience and opinions; it shouldn't be surprising that Reardon's situation is the one that mirrors Gissing's (some of Reardon's complaints about feeling blocked are drawn directly from Gissing's diary). Born in Wakefield, England, in 1857 to a chemist and his wife, Gissing excelled in school at least partly out of spite toward his peers. His studies and early writing earned him scholarships and prizes that allowed him to attend the University of London, but he was expelled and jailed for stealing from other students – out of necessity, not spite. This put a serious wrench in what he had assumed would be his direct ascent to a leisurely and well-compensated life of the mind.

Upon his release, Gissing scrounged together enough money to move briefly to America, where he taught classics and wrote short stories well enough to be published by newspapers and to have one of his stories stolen by another, less scrupulous publisher. He did not make enough from this to set himself up, and so after a brief stint as a travelling salesman, he spent some time in Germany before returning to England. Though his itinerant period was marked by distinct poverty – he survived for a while only on literal peanuts – back in England he found steady work as a teacher and tutor, reading classics and writing in his spare time. Gissing claimed this period also left him destitute, but his (few) friends told a different story: he was in enough demand that he could have lived quite comfortably, he just considered the work beneath him and would complain about it taking away from his true vocation.

However he felt about it, this life did eventually get him to where he wanted to be. He published his first three-volume novel at the age of twenty-three, and by the time *New Grub Street* came out, he was able to live entirely off his writing – just not well enough to ever feel satisfied. He partially blamed his soon-to-be-ex wife, who he accused, both personally and indirectly in *New Grub Street*, of not understanding his work and wanting to stay with him only if he became richer and more successful, an accusation that might have had more weight if he hadn't also accused his first wife of the same. Despite being able to live and travel around Europe in reasonable comfort, if not extravagance, while publishing more than a dozen other works of fiction and non-fiction – including studies of his hero, Dickens, and the well-regarded novel *The Odd Women*, which shows considerably more understanding of the nascent feminist movement than he seems to have shown his wives – Gissing lived the rest of his life in a persistent state of dissatisfaction. At the time of Gissing's death, at forty-five, his friend H. G. Wells lamented his 'poor vexed brain –so competent for learning and aesthetic reception, so incompetent, so impulsive and weakly yielding under the real stresses of life.'

Gissing had enough talent and intelligence to live as free a life as any artist. It never proved enough. He never attained the freedom that he knew the money he deserved, the way he deserved it, would have bought him.

———

A whole other interlocking web of repressions and social strictures contributed to Gissing's generalized dissatisfaction, and while we've come some way from the rest of the Victorian bullshit, where we get our money and what it means for our social standing hasn't changed all that much, even if some of the trappings are different. Minus the self-loathing, Gissing's general idea about what makes someone a true artist is fairly widespread: if you do not make a living through your art – the type of living that puts you on equal or better socio-economic footing with your presumed audience, or at least lifts you up above your origins – it doesn't really count. It's a side gig or a dream or a hobby, but it's not being an artist. A plumber is someone who makes their money from plumbing; an artist is someone who makes their money from art.

This is, of course, delusional if you have spent any time in artistic circles at any point after the age of maybe twenty-five or so, when 'other jobs' become less of a waypoint and more a permanent feature. (Which is not to say plenty of people, including a lot of artists, don't practise the delusion for a long time after.) The reality of artistic production is that the overwhelming majority of people who are making art in some capacity have to do something else to get by. Most of them, quite thankfully, are a little more sanguine about it, at least most of the time. But it's a vocation, not necessarily a living. Or at least, not enough of one.

———

Definitive statistics about how artists spend their time are hard to come by, for a myriad of reasons. Almost all of them rely on self-reporting, which is a wide and chaotic net, but the bigger issue is that it's rare for such studies to measure things the same way, especially when we consider definitions. One study will count a primary occupation based on hours spent, another will consider it in terms of percentage of income; one considers any related aspect of work in a creative field to count toward 'full-time' work in that field, another specifies that it is only the creation and/or display of art that counts, and yet another also allows time for business administration (which seems fair, given how many artists are effectively freelance contractors, even if they have established connections).

This doesn't even get into the wild disparities in how various artistic practices function: performing artists like actors and dancers, even the relative few who don't need to fill in the gaps, tend to have short periods of intensive work with fallow periods in between, whereas people who can work on their creations whenever, like writers and visual artists, tend to do their work more slowly and steadily, and musicians fall somewhere in the middle of that spectrum. And then there's the matter of exactly when and how work is paid for, which can render statistical snapshots somewhat meaningless: at least one study noted that, for at least half the people who self-identify as artists, both income from and time spent on creative work can vary by as much as 50 percent, depending on which period you're actually measuring – say, if they actually have a gig or not. And for at least half those people, artistic life is a truly all-or-nothing affair: they can go from spending all their time and making all their money from their artistic pursuits in one year to spending no time and making nothing from it the following year. Someone hasn't necessarily ceased being an artist if they got a grant, a prize, and a fellowship one year and then had to spend the next year on a contract to cover the gap until their work got released.

You also have to purposefully ignore that about half the information in these studies on artists' income or occupation is from trade groups that are making arguments for why their members should get more money from somewhere, anywhere. This can lead to somewhat fuzzy methods and interpretations. I'm not so slavishly devoted to Truth that I'm going to get uppity about people arguing for more money for artists, and they're not really wrong so much as trying to measure things that don't particularly lend themselves to easy measuring. Purely academic studies tend to be more objective, but statistics from government departments tend to paint a rosier picture, largely because they often don't count anyone who isn't making a pretty good portion of their money from artistic endeavour – and they also sometimes count money made from non-artistic endeavours by people who are also paid for artistic endeavours. That makes some sense when your goal is to measure economic activity, but it really, really does not reflect how people actually engage with making art. You don't measure the health of an education system by measuring the income of valedictorians.

So direct comparison is difficult, but some general trends stick out across the various methods, institutions, and even years. The highest proportion of artists who claim to be 'working full-time in their creative field,' in any study I've seen, is about 40 percent, but that includes people who do things like, say, teach private lessons or in degree programs, or who buttress their music-performing careers with things like audio engineering or production – all absolutely relevant to their creative field, but not at all allowing exclusive devotion to the creation (or even administration) of work. A better estimate is somewhere between about 10 and 20 percent who exclusively do the thing their artist bios say they do, with performance-based artists on the lower end, and those who do not necessarily need to be physically present to earn a cheque on the higher. The latter will take the odd speaking engagement or workshop mentorship or other one-shot gig, but generally speaking somewhere above three-quarters of their time or income is directly spent on/earned from art and art-making, which seems like a fair-enough cut-off.

———

There's a tendency in both the general public and the art world to assume that this breakdown is getting worse, but it has seemed to stay broadly constant since maybe the Enlightenment. Not a lot of trade groups did studies back then, admittedly, but there's enough anecdotal evidence even from the few artists whose names have survived to suggest that splitting time has long been the norm, except for a very rarified few. Individual artistic professions will wax and wane as their mediums grow or shrink in popularity, and the rise of mechanical distribution methods seems to have pushed this to a peak in the mid-twentieth century. But our perception of how easy it is to get by is largely survivorship bias: with the notable but very tiny exception of the famous few who weren't widely appreciated until after they died, if your art or reputation has managed to persist across decades or centuries, it's probably because you were notable enough in your own day to at some point devote yourself exclusively to making stuff.

The science-fiction author John Scalzi has an illustrative anecdote about this. He was once talking to a representative of the Authors Guild who was lamenting how much tougher it is for modern authors. The Guild member noted that people like Faulkner, Hemingway, and Cheever could make solid middle-class livings solely off writing fiction. As Scalzi pointed out, the fact that two-thirds of them are literally Nobel Prize winners does not exactly make them a representative sample of working writers. (And even Faulkner had to go to Hollywood to get by, which was still creative work but work he didn't think much of, and anyway, that isn't what we're celebrating him for here.)

Though I feel fairly comfortable saying he's not going to be up for the Nobel Prize any time soon, I wouldn't try to predict how long Scalzi's work may last in the popular consciousness. But his own career stands as a far better example of how one actually makes a middle-class living on full-time fiction writing: by his own admission, he's been a 'full-time author' for only about ten of the thirty or so years he's been trying to publish fiction; he worked as a newspaper reporter and columnist, an online editor, an author of Rough Guides, and, primarily, as a freelance corporate consultant before he managed to set those aside after multiple award nominations and bestsellers, some of which he has expressly admitted were written because he thought they would be more marketable. He likely owes his continued spot in the 20 percent to his ability to write fiction by the pound, having published pretty much a book a year for the last fifteen, and he still supplements this work with magazine articles, freelance columns, and consulting on video games, and he was one of the original writers to cultivate an online presence. This may lack the romance of drunkenly typing terse sentences while standing at a typewriter, but even with a particularly blessed career, Scalzi has vastly more in common with the standard professionalish writer of the last century or two than anyone who is on a last-name basis with the whole of literate society. To the degree that this is a problem, it's been a perpetual one.

Which is the main point here: there's plenty to criticize in how the modernish world appreciates and compensates artists and/or people in general, but it seems to have found an equilibrium on what rough percentage of people can solely devote themselves to art. I don't know that you could say it's fair or good, exactly, but it's at least consistent.

———

The popular conception of a side gig is something like the actor who spends their days waiting tables or the musician who fixes leaks between jam sessions. Virtually everyone who is not a household name before their twenty-first birthday has some kind of story of a job like this. Maybe the most famous modern anecdote in this vein involves the composer Philip Glass. Despite training at Juilliard and getting a Fulbright Scholarship en route to becoming maybe the most celebrated American composer since John Philip Sousa, Glass spent the first fifteen years of his career employed as a taxi driver and plumber. Once, while he was installing a dishwasher, the owner of the house, *Time* magazine art critic Robert Hughes, stopped him to exclaim, 'But you're Philip Glass! What are you doing here?' In Glass's words, 'I explained that I was an artist but that I was sometimes a plumber as well, and that he should go away and let me finish.'

That a thirty-nine-year-old Glass continued to drive a cab even after the premiere of his masterwork opera, *Einstein on the Beach*, puts some lie to the equally popular conception that jobs like these are exclusively for those who are failing at being artists (although Glass did eventually retire to focus exclusively on music and general renown). Even the idea that less heady jobs in service or trades are the most common form of moonlighting for artists is way off: according to a 2013 National Endowment for the Arts study, which is pretty much in line with other explorations of the subject, better than half of people who work as artists but can't (or don't) make it their full-time job are employed in professional fields – which is to say, things that require some form of degree or credential. Even eliminating the more than half of those who work as teachers – whether specifically as some form of art teacher or in more generalized education roles – professional is still the next most likely gig, nearly double the next nearest classifications: management/financial (also professions that require more qualifications than a warm body, ostensibly), service, and sales.

All of which is to say that the vast majority of the people who work significantly enough as artists to meet the institutional criteria are not splitting their time between the rarified air of the art world and the simplest job they could get their hands on. They are paying their bills with professions that in many cases require a nominally full-time commitment (that's debatable with stuff like the modern email job, but those require a pretty ceaseless amount of hoop-jumping, whether that's acquiring credentials or just beating the productivity software).

Maybe the most extreme example are the physicians who somehow find time in between reading medical books to write a few books themselves. Many of the more notable doctor/writers gave up the profession before they dove into writing – early-twentieth-century Russian novelist Mikhail Bulgakov wrote his classic short story cycle *A Young Doctor's Notebook* half a decade after giving up the profession and the morphine addiction the stories explore – but there is still a bevy of people happy to make you look like a slovenly piece of shit for not penning literary classics between saving lives. William Carlos Williams published his first book of poetry three years after graduating from medical school, and by the time he was apologizing for stealing plums, he had been head of a pediatrics department for nearly a decade. (He also wrote short stories and a book literally called *The Great American Novel*, which, I mean, Jesus Christ, and no wonder he didn't have time to buy his own fruit.) Egyptian feminist writer Nawal El Saadawi is better known for her non-fiction polemics and political advocacy but still managed to write twenty novels and short story collections while working as a doctor and public health administrator and being chased out of those roles and her home country on account of her politics. Canadian author Vincent Lam finished his Giller Prize–winning short story collection, *Bloodletting & Other Miraculous Cures*, while working as an emergency room physician and has since transferred to the mildly less stressful role of working at an addictions clinic in the midst of a national addictions crisis, which formed the basis for his second novel, 2023's *On the Ravine*.

———

Far more common among professional jobs in the last century or so is something at least mildly related to some of the knowledge and skills an artist might employ: advertising. Adjacent to that are professions that exist to draw attention to stuff that multinational corporations spend billions upon billions to make you think about: call these workers communications staff or design professionals or even the creative class, if you like, but they are fundamentally the foot soldiers of the progressively expanding attention economy.

And wouldn't you know it, making art and getting people's attention have a lot of overlap.

Since the rise of commercial text and images, there has been a stigma about using one's artistic gifts for commercial purposes. The 1990s alternative music/film scene might be the most recent popular expression of this disdain, but eighty years earlier, Ukrainian avant-gardist Kazimir Malevich was sufficiently ashamed of his work designing a perfume bottle and advertisements for Russian company Brocard – undertaken only because he was desperately broke, and giving him the stability to start producing work like *Black Square*, one of the first modernist images – that he managed to keep it a secret from all but his family until after his death. Salvador Dalí's contemporaries accused him of degrading his talent with his semi-frequent commercial work. Dashiell Hammett, who wrote ad copy when he wasn't penning some of the world's most celebrated detective stories, felt the need to defend his other profession in an essay called 'The Advertisement IS Literature,' noting that both the novelist and the copywriter 'must set his idea on the paper in such form that it will have the effect he desires on those who read it.' But whether they approve of advertising work or not, morals cost more than many artists can afford, and most artists who have taken a cheque from an advertising firm are not so much trading off their good, established name as taking whatever job is available, ads being all the better for the fact that no separate training is required.

———

I feel it would be going much, much too far to credibly claim that ads are art, even if they employ the same techniques, but some artists have been able to stretch their creative legs within the bounds of selling stuff, or at least got someone else to pay them to develop techniques or ideas that they later put to their own uses. This was virtually the origin story of pop art, although I think some of this tension is better illustrated by a figure like Dora Maar, most famous for her association with Picasso but steadily becoming more appreciated in her own right. Maar established herself in Paris as a photographer of surrealist images, politically inflected portraits of the poor in Depression-era America, and plenty of fashion and commercial work, the mix of which seemed to bother her far less than did any of Picasso's depictions of her.

Born in 1907 as Henriette Theodora Markovitch to a noted Parisian architect, Maar changed her name when she went to art school at the age of nineteen, possibly to downplay the connection to her father, who helped fund her studies and her studios in her twenties. She was an absolute gadfly; one of the recent reclamation projects, a 2020 book by journalist Brigitte Benkemoun, tells her life story through her address book, which is packed to the brim with notable Parisian artists of the time – she learned from Henri Cartier-Bresson, hung out with André Breton and Jacqueline Lamba, and met her first business partner, Pierre Kefer, hanging around early film sets. Founding a studio together in 1930, she and Kefer did commercial shoots for the likes of Chanel and *Le Figaro*, becoming successful enough that she was able to live primarily off the work she did through the thirties for most of the rest of her life. Surrealist art found its way into her commercial work: one of her most notable shots, *The Years Lie in Wait for You*, of a spider-webbed portrait of a woman grabbing her face, reportedly began as a face cream advertisement before being repurposed. She gradually expanded her repertoire to include deeply leftist street photographs and outright surrealism, before all but giving up photography entirely at the behest and bullying of Picasso. She turned to painting, but little of that art was exhibited until after her death, her talent overshadowed and her mental health wavering after her dalliance with the 'morally worthless' man. When her contemporaries weren't reducing her to the muse for the 'Weeping Woman' paintings, they noted she was a commercial photographer before she began sitting for Picasso.

———————

There might not be a more natural, if also more fraught, complementary profession to artistry than criticism. Who, after all, would have a better perspective on the necessary background and unique challenges of making art than someone who does it themselves? But – considering everything from personal bias (if you don't do it the way I do it, it can't be worth doing) to the prospect of blowing up personal relationships (and maybe future commissions) – it can be deluded or even dangerous to offer your opinion for public consumption.

If we blur the line between philosophical aesthetic theory and popular critique, artists have been moonlighting as critics since the earliest days that the former category congealed. Plenty of Greek and Roman philosophy treats what we'd now call aesthetic theory as a crucial component of our conception of the world, although its overall project doesn't really line up with our conception of what constitutes art. Those philosophers are better considered the forebears of the more august tradition of criticizing stuff without doing it first. (Which I wholeheartedly support, I must say, at least when you're willing to think deeply about it.)

The earliest artist-critics we know about tend to come from outside Western traditions. The author of the *Nāṭyaśāstra*, which gave us the Indian concept of rasa – the emotional essence of a piece, the je ne sais quoi that moves us – is unknown, and might have been multiple people across many years, but that text was written in a distinctly poetic form that suggests it was the work of a practitioner.

Xie He was a sixth-century Chinese painter and writer whose only surviving work is *The Record of the Classification of Old Painters*, which includes his framework for understanding painting, the Six Principles. More than a millennium before Western aesthetic theory caught up, this engaged with the debate about craft versus art: 'Even if the artist is skillful, he will not be able to elevate himself above an ordinary crafts-man. Their art will be called painting, but in fact it will not be a true art. The Spirit Resonance is a gift of heavens, a natural talent one is born with. It pours straight out of one's soul.' The Arabic prince and poet Abdallah ibn al-Mu'tazz wrote a consideration of poetry, *Kitab al-Badi*, in the ninth century, some time before his one-day reign as leader of the Abbasid Caliphate. (He was strangled to death, though it was a political matter, not the vengeance of an angry poet.) Both of those works, though, were more pure exercises of the mind than ways to make ends meet: Xie would have been painting only as a function of his post as civil servant in the Confucianist tradition, and al-Mu'tazz's only worldly concern was political enemies.

Our more modern and cravenly capitalistic criticism has its strongest roots in the eighteenth century. Jonathan Rich-ardson the Elder apprenticed under John Riley, the court painter of English king William of Orange and made a fine living as a portrait painter of various nobles and notables throughout the first half of the 1700s. He struck gold, though, with several books on how to appreciate painting written in the 1710s and '20s, most notably *An Essay on the Theory of Painting* and *An Essay on the Whole Art of Criticism* (the latter is one of the first recorded uses of the word *criticism*). Though somewhat prosaic, even compared to Xie's work – Richardson detailed his own eighteen-point scale in seven separate categories to determine the 'worth' of a painting – it proved hugely popular with the burgeoning middle and merchant classes, who had enough money to buy paintings, just like the nobles they were trying to emulate, but not necessarily enough to hire experts and advisers.

There is and has been considerable tension about the extent to which criticism is a serious consideration of art and its effect on the soul – the extent to which it is an art in and of itself – and its place as a sort of de facto *Consumer's Guide*. In the early days, it was a pretty pure creature of commerce. In England and France, with the rise of pamphlets and papers that spoke expressly to a middle-class audience, criticism became a decent way to earn a living for anyone who knew a bit about painting and could string a few words together. As with modern criticism, it didn't hurt if you also knew how to play to your audience: the earliest surviving critique of the Parisian Salon, the annual exhibition of French Royal Academy painters, is an anonymous pamphlet that includes a fairly lengthy denigration of the nobles who attended and praises the general public for being far more savvy about good art. Not that nobles weren't also interested in help with their taste: in his later life, the French polymath Diderot sustained himself partly on reviews of the Salon in the 1760s and '70s for *La Correspondance littéraire, philosophique et critique*. The fact that reviews in general and the *Correspondance* in particular were banned in France and so sent abroad also helped raise his international profile, eventually leading to sustained support from Catherine the Great.

But it was newspapers and periodicals that gradually became the main outlet for artistic criticism, and once the practice became established enough that writers ceased using pseudonyms (to limit blowback from negative reviews) and stopped accepting 'gifts' from subjects, criticism of various forms of art became a reliable way to make a name and a crust. William Hazlitt spent his twenties as a portrait painter, and though he grew frustrated with his self-diagnosed lack of talent and unwillingness to paint more flattering portraits of the rich people who were paying him, his studies helped him immensely when he was hired as a reporter. He transitioned quickly to critical reviews of painting, then literary works, indulging in both throughout his eventual career as one of the more celebrated essayists in the English language. (I worked for a time for an outlet that bears his name, although I hadn't heard of him before they hired me. Apologies to William and all involved in my hiring.)

———

Perhaps the person who had the most lasting impact on both criticism and his preferred art form, though, was Charles Baudelaire. Presumably no one who gets adjectivized needs too much of an introduction, but luckily for our purposes, in addition to being hailed as an age-defining genius of criticism and poetry, he was absolute shit with money, which seemed to contribute to his critical output almost as much as his burning desire to explain why everyone else was wrong about the world.

Born in 1821, Baudelaire came from a fairly well-off family. His father died when Charles was only six, and his stepfather eventually became an ambassador, which set his mother up for life. Some part of Baudelaire's lifelong free-spending and indolence seems to be a direct rebellion against the man, if not outright Freudian jealousy – Charles was an unabashed mama's boy. He was encouraged to go into law or diplomacy like the step-old-man but decided to be a writer upon getting the 1800s equivalent of a trust fund when he was twenty-one. He blew through it quite quickly, and the rest of his life was a cycle of waiting for semi-lucrative writing work to come his way, moving to avoid creditors, and begging his mother for money. She didn't love that: 'Oh, what grief,' his mother once wrote. 'If Charles had let himself be guided by his stepfather … he would not have left a name in literature, it is true, but we should have been happier.' Might put your own mother asking how that screenplay is coming into a little more perspective.

Baudelaire's first works to attract serious attention were reviews of the 1845 and 1846 Salons, which, besides being both vivacious and occasionally vicious, preceded (and argu-ably inspired) the Impressionists' critiques of the Academy by about thirty years – not that he would live to see them borne out. In these reviews he established his method of responding viscerally to the work, rendering literal descrip-tion of the paintings secondary to the feelings and thoughts the work evoked in him. Though these tendencies would flourish in his later criticism – especially 1863's 'The Painter of Modern Life,' a consideration of his friend Constantin Guys that was published in *Le Figaro* and in which he invented the term 'modernity' – the template he provided for modern criti-cism was established basically from the hop.

He published criticism more or less continuously from then on – when he was in the mood to write at all – but a decade later his reputation as a critic was overshadowed by the publication of *Les Fleurs du Mal* (ironically, the same year his stepfather died), parts of which he had been working on since his money first came in. An unsparing but vividly beautiful look at sex, mortality, melancholy, and the bleak harshness of then-modern Parisian life, the poetry book thrilled artists almost as much as it offended the general public. Baudelaire and his publisher were prosecuted and fined for offending public morality, and several poems were outright banned, removed from later editions. This didn't hurt his reputation as a bold new voice, but it definitely didn't help his ability to not hold on to money.

Baudelaire died a decade after *Les Fleurs du Mal*'s release. He was witness to some of the impact it would have – Victor Hugo came to his public defence – and his reputation grew posthumously to the point that Rimbaud, Proust, and Eliot all credited him as the finest poet of his era. His increasing notoriety did not help his finances or his work ethic, though he had a brief period of security and relative productivity when his mother allowed him to move back in with her in 1859. Besides criticism, prose poetry, and translation, he wrote a consideration of being an opium and hashish user, and he decided to live that life more fully, mixed in with heavy drinking and a light wallet, when he moved to Brussels in 1864. Less than two years later, he suffered a debilitating stroke, and he spent the last year of his life semi-paralyzed and unable to speak. Upon his death, his mother settled his rather voluminous debts and eventually came to peace with his place in literature.

However scattered his life, Baudelaire's professional work has a gem-like unity. There is profound sympathy between his criticism and his poetry – including an almost fanatical obsession with drawing out the beauty of this thing in front of him, life or art, regardless of prevailing opinion – but his ability to push both of those forms in new directions seems almost impossible, with the vantage of hindsight. Art and criticism are not quite as spiritually opposed as some artists in particular like to imagine: they are at base attempts to pin down something ineffable, and as Baudelaire himself shows, a sharp and careful eye, a historical knowledge, and a gift for descriptive detail, in whatever medium, serve both very well. With that said, the base impulse of art is to capture this spirit without necessarily explaining it, to reveal the energy that vibrates through the fluttering of a butterfly's wings; criticism is more concerned with pinning down the butterfly and figuring out how it works. Both can help you feel the full extent of what a butterfly means, but arriving at the same place doesn't mean taking the same road.

Consider this passage from 'The Painter of Modern Life,' wherein Baudelaire explains what he means by modernity, and why his friend seems to embody it:

He strives, for his own part, to extract from the fashionable whatever it may contain of the poetical within the historical, to draw the eternal from the transitory… It is easier to decide, at the outset, that everything about the modes of dress of an epoch is ugly, rather than applying oneself to extracting from it the mysterious beauty it might perhaps contain, however minimal or slight that might be. Modernity is the transitory, the fugitive, the contingent, that half of art of which the other is the eternal and immutable.

The passage is precise, clear, and energetic. It's convincing partly because it's so invigorating, and there's no doubting what it is we can or should do with the information here. It's an argument, probably not totally rational, but on the spectrum. Baudelaire's criticism has been accused, not unfairly, of being inconsistent, and at times it seems more like he is writing about what he wants to see – dreaming of Impressionism, maybe – than what is in front of him. Summing up the consensus, academic Sara Pappas says he 'does not simply privilege the new in his art critical writings; he creates a kind of absolute originality through his writings that is not actually present in the art of the period in the way that he theorizes.'

But I think this inconsistency is not just part of the originality that made him so important; it's part of what separates criticism, especially after Baudelaire, from a more academic aesthetic theory. Baudelaire is not really evaluating things along a framework; he's responding to what he sees and feels in the moment; any consistency is down to the bounds of his temperament, his ideas of the world. It's a part of the 'spirit resonance' that Xie He talked about, the vitality of the work. Any grander idea or narrative is emergent, not restrained to a purely rational or logical conception. His criticism is as consistent and considered as his moods and feelings – just pinned down and (often beautifully) articulated. Baudelaire's poetry has the same tendency, without the pins.

———

Baudelaire had no shortage of impediments to writing, but I have to wonder if some of his slow and scattered process wasn't due to balancing these competing impulses (or running away from them entirely when he couldn't find any balance). As an organizing principle, the context required of good criticism is almost antithetical to good art: if the latter is about capturing the specificity of a vision or feeling, the former is about fitting those feelings in, finding their place, and weighing them against each other. It can be utterly paralyzing to commit to your vision if you are confronted with its wider context. Comparison becomes the thief of joy: Why should you make anything when this thing and that thing and this other thing are all expressing the same feeling? What is the point of words that seem lesser than the genius who inspired you to write them? And if your work cannot find its wider place, if it does seem unique in viewpoint or execution, does that mean that you're so far beyond the realm of sense or worth that no one else will ever get any value from it?

If Baudelaire ever felt those things, he got over them eventually ('I know that this book,' he wrote to his mother in the midst of the public backlash, in what is a spectacular act of either confidence or conciliatory bluster, 'with its virtues and its faults, will make its way in the memory of the lettered public, beside the best poems of Hugo, Gautier and even Byron'). But that it took a world historical genius to overcome those things is an indication of the danger of this particular gig as a sideline. The inherent danger of spending too much time on anything other than art is that it will dull whatever sensitivity or instinct allows you to make something in the first place. Maybe doubly so when your other job is examining that instinct so closely you might just need to kill it to understand it.

I don't mean to be dramatic. Maybe I just mean to justify my own slow and laborious, though less debauched, process. Certainly plenty of people after Baudelaire have also navigated this conundrum, with (for the most part) less opium use and Freudian begging. One of the purest expressions of the Baudelairean tendency emerged in the 1950s and '60s in the magazine *ARTnews*, which hired a gaggle of poets from what would become known as the New York School to review the modern art scene. Poets like Randall Jarrell, Frank O'Hara, and John Ashbery – who for the most part never made even a middle-class living publishing poetry, even in this apparently glorious age for writing-to-pay-the-bills – found a perfect subject in the abstract expressionism and pop art that came into vogue: a talent for succinct evocation, or just the inherent music of words, helped a lot when they were tasked with responding to colour fields or a repurposed bed with paint on it.

Like Baudelaire's, these reviews tended to be, if not always light on descriptive detail, less concerned with telling you what a thing looked like and more with capturing the impression it left. In a review of a Robert Rauschenberg show, the not-yet-Pulitzer-winner John Ashbery said of one of the collages that it 'does not have the "Step along, please" feeling of a Schwitters collage … You also have the artist's permission to get nothing out of looking at his paintings other than the marginal pleasure of being alive.' That would fit right in with some of Ashbery's purposefully poetic work, which also tends to eschew grandiose language or description for perfectly punctuated plain profundity. 'The marginal pleasure of being alive' carries enough weight to justify a book, let alone a magazine. (Most certainly out of necessity, Ashbery kept up his reviews and editing in outlets like *New*

York, Newsweek, and the *Partisan Review* even after *Self-Portrait in Convex Mirror* won the Pulitzer in 1975.)

Around the same time, there was a vogue for the relatively nascent field of film criticism to provide a haven for aspiring or moonlighting filmmakers. The French New Wave and the critical journal *Cahiers du Cinéma* essentially grew up together, and in America Martin Scorsese led the charge of film-school brats roping in film-critic brats to bring a little more depth to Hollywood: both Paul Schrader (*Taxi Driver,* etc.) and Jay Cocks (*Gangs of New York*) got their start reviewing movies for papers and magazines before they wrote some of the landmark American movies of the twentieth century. They maybe shouldn't entirely count, though: in the economics of film-making in the late twentieth century, these people rather quickly got into the rarified 20 percent who earn their living solely from art – criticism was a stepping stone, not a lifelong ping-pong act. I bring them up more because film might be the last art form to support criticism as a sensible sideline. The future for one of the most artistic of side gigs does not look especially bright.

Some of the cultural forces rendering criticism moot are closely related to the problems facing academia and journalism. A general disinterest in anything an MBA does not consider immediately practical, and the financialization and attendant hollowing-out of legitimate institutions, isn't good for anyone who wants to make art, much less think about it.

But at the risk of seeming phenomenally gullible – when I started researching this book in earnest in the fall of 2022, it really seemed like I was going to have to have a section on National Film and Television School, which *hahahahaha* – the most unique and pressing threat to criticism as a full- or side-time profession seems to be artificial intelligence.

There are at least three serious-ish threats that AI presents to art generally, one of which is a particularly acute problem for criticism: in rough order of seriousness, I would describe those as AI taking over the making of art, AI taking over the art-adjacent side gigs that inherently support artists, and AI-inflected algorithmic recommendation taking over how art is discovered and publicly appreciated.

Before I get into these, I feel the need to point out that I have vanishingly little interest in AI art as it currently stands. Some people seem to be seriously pursuing whatever potential may exist in it, but the vast majority of it seems to be a shortcut for people who lack the curiosity or willingness to learn and persevere that we take for granted in children. I don't think struggle is necessary to art, but a basic interest in developing a skill certainly is, primarily because that is how you begin to understand the meaning and effect of the choices you make while creating something. Even if we limit ourselves to the somewhat established or devoted artists who are exploring AI's boundaries, their willingness to overlook the outright theft of massive libraries of creative work strikes me as naive at best and outright disrespectful at a minimum. I'm not overly precious about my copyright; someone using my work as inspiration to create something for themselves is as valuable to me as creating my own meaningful expression in the first place, even if I'm not credited or compensated. But that's hugely different than being just another data point in a system that lets people spew out mechanical nonsense. As far as I'm concerned, anyone who has used the current AI models for creative work should at minimum renounce any form of compensation or respect they accrue from it; even plagiarists and forgers have to actually interact with the thing they're copying first.

Maybe I'm too cynical about the lofty claims of tech evangelists or too optimistic about why people choose to consume and experience the art they do, but AI-generated art doesn't seem like too serious a threat to artists, primarily because, now and for the foreseeable future, it can't actually do the essential stuff of creation: having an idea, and making the choices that convey that idea. Without falling too far down an aesthetical rabbit hole, at least since the critic Arthur Danto coined the term 'Artworld' – and for decades before that, at minimum – the straightforward ability to actually make a thing hasn't been the most important factor for determining what is art, let alone good art. To stick roughly to Danto's time frame, the mid-1960s, think about the most cynical reaction to the scribbling brushstrokes or plain colour fields of abstract expressionism (or even Malevich's *Black Square*): 'I/my kid could paint that!' Which, of course – but the scribbles or colours aren't the whole of the point: the idea of presenting scribbles or colours as a painting is. These are art – noteworthy and talked-about art – because the artist has synthesized some combination of historical knowledge, artistic technique, and their own interior state into an interesting (if sometimes maybe insular) statement about the world. Slapping up your own scribbles could, it's true, also constitute a statement, but 'the techniques of some art aren't that hard to do' is a pretty facile thought: no one thinks you could have written *Hamlet* just because you wrote an email, though the techniques are pretty much the same.

AI doesn't as yet have any ideas: all those are entirely at the whim of the person writing the prompt. We have already had AI art attract some attention: for instance, Japanese author Rie Qudan won the Akutagawa Prize, an award given to rising literary talents, for *Tokyo-to Dojo-to*, a book she admits was partially written by ChatGPT. But this only reveals the extent to which AI is a tool, not a rising talent: even if she didn't edit or elide any of its outputs, Qudan gave it direction and shape, judged its contributions against her desires, and put everything into place. There's maybe an argument to separate this technique out from what we traditionally consider 'writing' a 'novel,' but it doesn't strike me as substantially different from, say, found poetry. Or, for that matter, Photoshop, which is also a digital tool that allows artists to easily do technically difficult things they might not otherwise be able to pull off – surrealist images like Maar's, for instance, are absurdly trivial to make these days – and is so widespread across visual arts now as to not rate a mention in the 'medium' section of most art labels. As long as there's a human hand guiding the process, there will be one to accept the cheque (or, I guess, click Accept on the digital transfer).

A more properly human-y AI that directs itself may be possible, in which case artists getting paid is probably going to be a bit of a second-order problem. Art doesn't come with a scoreboard: like all art made by a conscious being, it will be judged based on how well it represents and expands our own thoughts and feelings, and that will vary tremendously with the person. Maybe an AI would be massively more productive, but plenty of our human artists show that volume is not necessarily a path to repute. And again: if a purely synthetic being decides to exclusively devote itself to becoming the most celebrated literary mind since Shakespeare, well, that's gotta count as a win, if some of the human-created stories about AI are accurate guesses about what it might do.

———

A much bigger problem would seem to me to come in the form of what AI might mean for arts-adjacent professions. Photoshop (or at least the full Adobe Creative Suite and its online capabilities) is a pretty instructive example: it has not ended art as we know it, but it did destroy an awful lot of jobs that directly supported artists, either in the production of work or as a source of income for the artists while they did other things. Whether through the obsolescence of entire professions or reduction in the amount of labour required to do a commonplace thing – the modern graphic designer does not need to spend much of their time, say, drawing their own pictures or lettering, let alone physically making and delivering a product – there have been material impacts to artists if not to their art.

AI is not exactly breaking new ground on this front: speaking of the internet, things like Fiverr, which essentially expedited the process of undercutting your peers, are already doing a great job of pushing the efficiencies of the previous round of digital tools to their material limits. But there's plenty of proof that, even if they might want some humanity in their art galleries, no one with money seems to give a shit about any part of the money-making process. Again, current AI tools still need some kind of minder, and probably will for the foreseeable future, but if you don't even need a contract stock photographer to get images that appear to be people doing things, and one prompt engineer with a Photoshop certificate can pump out as many ads as four graphic designers with BAs, it's a safe bet that five people will be out of a job (multiplied by the thousands of different firms running this math). I'm not sure what the magic ratio is of extant professional jobs to people with enough financial security to make decent art, but I do know that not even our aging population will need that many doctors.

For a critic, the final problem, algorithmic recommendation, ratchets up the efficiency to existential levels. Though criticism has, almost from the point it first congealed into a sensible profession, constituted vastly more than a buyer's guide, the economic case for any kind of broad support hasn't necessarily gone any deeper than that. And if there's one thing machine learning has plainly figured out well enough that the vast majority doesn't notice the difference, it's how to tell you that, if you like this, you'll probably like that.

My experience with these sorts of recommendation algorithms tends to show the seams, if not burst them fully. Maybe because I'm mildly resistant to embracing the thumbs, hearts, and stars that they ask for, I find these are spectacularly good at juuuuust missing the point enough to be really annoying: 'Oh, you like whiny, excessively literate nerd-boys singing technically on tune but definitely outside the realm of actually pleasant? Well, here are four more that are too nasal and whose verse construction is obviously too precious by half.' It's like asking a robot to build a three-bedroom house, and then it does, but none of the rooms have windows and the kitchen is in the garage.

There are a few caveats here. It seems obvious, based on subscription numbers for these various platforms, that I am in the minority. I am also still of an age where I can remember when actively searching things out was the only way to find them, first in a physical copy and then through a blog roll, RSS feed, and downloading and organizing things. It doesn't seem too hard to imagine that subsequent generations, unmoored from even that relatively easy process, will never even be aware of what they are missing, let alone think to miss it and seek it out. I don't think it's only nostalgia that makes me think we will lose something crucial if no one is ever stumbling upon or being directed to a book or record or film that their previous consumption never would have predicted; some of my most powerful experiences of art are the result of either happenstance or giving a critic the benefit of the doubt, the kind of true serendipity that a weighted average will always miss but a trusted voice who isn't trying to cater to me will produce as a matter of course.

Whatever my misgivings, I still let these recommendation engines drive, poorly, almost as often as I purposefully seek out genuinely new things. For most people they're doing the job just fine. If they get a bit better, or people like me care a bit less, or media consolidation wipes out a few more critical outlets, that might be enough for an entire genre of arguably artistic output – criticism – to be reduced to a hobby or curio. Maybe there will still be some people who pursue it, and some people who are obsessive enough about it to financially support it, but it will be so obscure and difficult it will fully become an art, in the sense of the financial pressures and the absolute rarity of anyone being able to make a living off of it, but without the basic affinity or capitalist promotion that at least some art gets. It's hard to imagine buying popcorn to see Roger Ebert.

If criticism is the inversely adjacent sideline to life as an artist, the job most directly tied in to the making of art is, of course, teaching other people how to make it. The connection is so intertwined you could probably debate whether there is much in the way of meaningful distinction, and there's a strong case to be made that teaching can be as fruitful and worthwhile to an artist's actual creative process as, say, research. But let's not sell teaching short: as should be obvious to anyone who has actually learned something from a teacher, there is vastly more to it than simply showing someone with less experience what you know – even if plenty of people who teach don't rise much beyond that baseline requirement.

Across time and disciplines, becoming an artist has tended to involve extensive training, and generally the only people qualified to provide it are other artists, who have almost always been happy for the supplementary income. Outside of more generalized programs that included some artistic instruction, like the Chinese bureaucratic system or the modern public school – or the twentieth-century public school system, anyway – the most established lineage of training we have comes from the European visual arts. In the earliest days of people being considered artists, there was no way to paint or sculpt without apprenticing. In the fourteenth century, you would start with a guild, after which you might be able to learn in the workshop or studio of a master. Though, it should be said, most evidence suggests that the masters treated these as labour pools, not training grounds, and most of the learning you did at their feet would have been through your own careful attention. Eventually, the two ideas came together: in 1563, Cosimo de' Medici founded the Accademia e Compagnia delle Arti del Disegno (Academy and Company of the Arts of Drawing) in Florence, under the guidance of Giorgio Vasari. As the name implies, it was both a guild ('company') that represented the interests of its members, and an academy, made up of the most prominent artists, including Michelangelo, that oversaw production of all art, which included training people in the Florentine style. Florence being quite renowned for its art at the time, this was as much about protecting a brand as producing new artists, but the latter proved useful enough that the idea caught on, without the guild attached. Other academies opened across Italy in the sixteenth century, France and German-speaking areas in the seventeenth, and most of the rest of Europe in the eighteenth. True to form for the development of the concept of the artists, part of the rationale for this was to give a headier, more prestigious place to practise for the sensitive souls who had been brutalized (their words) by the guild system, although the practical upshot was the creation of a formal structure for students and teachers of art.

Talk about the teaching of art tends to focus on the student's perspective, for understandable reasons: there tend to be a lot more of them, and they tend to be the ones making substantial, life-altering decisions. Teachers are usually too far into their careers to be making decisions, and when they do it is probably more along the lines of choosing teaching over another, less attractive job. As someone who has had no formal education in any art above the high school level, I would not be terribly qualified to weigh in, nor is it really in the purview of this book, but there are two things worth saying. First, anyone who has made any sort of living as an artist, whether formally instructed or self-taught, has found significant amounts of time to train and hone their craft; insofar as structured education is just an excuse to do that, it's pretty valuable. Second, whatever the value of formal training in the arts might be, its contribution to the economy of the arts, to say nothing of the continued existence of working artists themselves, is pretty much invaluable.

There is absolutely no job that sustains artists like teaching. In almost any study, poll, or otherwise rigorous examination of the subject from about the 1970s on, about 20 to 25 percent of artists who do something other than art to pay their bills make the majority of their money from teaching. For another roughly 20 percent, that is how they spend the majority of their non-art-making time. Somewhere in the neighbourhood of two-thirds of working artists will have taught in formal programs – in academia, or at retreats, residencies, workshops, or private schools and studios – at some point in their careers. Outside of mass-market artistic pursuits like popular music, film, and television, it's likely even higher: since 2000, more than half of the winners of the Pulitzer Prize for Fiction, for instance, have had full-time jobs teaching at American universities, and several others spent at least a few years in the lead-up to the award on visiting professorships or teaching a class here or there. When the people at the head of your field are overwhelmingly teachers, you have left the territory of 'those who cannot do, teach' and entered into the realm of 'if you want to do, you best to learn how to teach, too.' Purely anecdotally, my publisher has several fun stories of being approached at various literary events by people who were looking to get their book published not necessarily because they wanted that particular work to find an audience but because it was a requirement to apply for a post-secondary teaching position.

(No doubt some truly meaningful work would pour out during their summers off.)

As implied by the sheer number of people who do it, teaching art has its advantages if your goal is to work as an artist. Going through formal training may not be necessary to becoming an artist, but people who have done it are familiar enough with the process to be able to turn around and teach. While it is rarely a lucrative career, it is a steadier one than virtually any artistic pursuit: even a Saturday-morning gig helping toddlers learn the basics of twirling can get you a solid eight to twelve weeks of paycheques at a go. Conversely, it can be flexible enough to provide a reasonable amount of time for your artistic practice or to accommodate irregular time demands: academic jobs offer a variety of sabbaticals, breaks, and even requirements for showing, publishing, or promoting work, whereas more gig-based teaching jobs can be picked up and dropped as the rest of your schedule dictates. Most importantly, teaching ensures you stay actively engaged with your medium. You get to see what the next generation of artists cares about; you have to engage with new styles, practices, and techniques. Helping students work through their own creative challenges can help you unlock your own. Someone else is paying you to think about art.

———

It is still a job, however. And even outside the more prosaic problems — ask anyone who teaches music how disheartening it is to see a full roster of students who haven't picked up their instrument in the week between lessons — there's plenty to suggest that teaching should not be or won't continue to be the solution it has been. The prevalence of teaching among artists can be seen as a benevolent subsidy, but the fact that so many have to do it is a problem. However sympathetic art-making and art-teaching are, they are entirely separate jobs with entirely different skill sets. The willingness to gloss over this fact affects the artists who get ground down and drained of their passion as much as it does the students who get thrown into the classes of people with no interest in trying to impart their skills beyond the paycheque. There is a reason virtually every other form of learning, especially at the more prestigious levels, requires people whose primary focus is on teaching.

Then there's the practical problem of an explosion of schools, degrees, and specialty training, especially at the highest levels. To take writing as one example, in 1994 there were sixty-four master of fine arts available in creative writing in America; today, there are over four hundred master's programs devoted solely to creative writing. Leaving aside the fact that, even with population growth, Americans are not reading six times more books than they were, this extensive proliferation has cheapened the very idea of meaningful, in-depth instruction. With the concurrent crisis in academia that has seen humanities budgets slashed and a serious rise in part-time, sessional, and adjunct teaching positions, there are theoretically more positions, but they offer much less in terms of security and pay compared to just, you know, writing. Piecing together work from these sorts of teaching positions can mean taking on excessive course loads, travelling between institutions, and needing further supplementary income from other sources entirely. In the case of someone teaching to support an artistic career, that means they need a side gig to their side gig. In concrete terms, it has meant the creation of an almost entirely separate industry that requires both aspiring and trained artists, without providing either group the prospect of meaningful work in the subject or the time to pursue their ostensible pursuits. We are planting vegetables so we can make better compost. (At least the teachers seem relatively safe from AI, for the time being.)

Still, the promise of teaching remains. It just seems mildly ironic that one of the few reliable foundations for an artistic career – one of the truly choice ways to fight against the fact that art, as a system, rewards relatively few people disproportionately – seems to be moulding itself into the same pyramidal shape. The vast majority of artists have always required some sort of side hustle. We don't know what future there will be if even the safest havens are just as brutally unforgiving as the art world itself. But if you're looking for an existential crisis in the arts, being unable to support yourself by teaching others to do it might be the purest one we have.

6: Art in the Time of the Content
Gazing into the Near Future

If money is a pollution of the creative spirit, then putting creative works in competition with each other is pure poison. The existence of some other, better work – even if it's solely you making that judgment – doesn't make the work that has resonated through you any less meaningful, whether you're creating or consuming it. Creativity – art – is a constantly expanding sum: every bit of it that we experience and appreciate and, especially, let into us helps everything that came before it grow and change, take on new shapes and dimensions, mean and seem like different things. You do not need to lock these things in a cage until one emerges victorious: they grow the world to fit their space.

Not that any society has ever actually acted like it had space for all of its art for any length of time. If the intrusion of material concerns on art is a consequence of the need to eat, the need to categorize, subjugate, and declare winners in art is some more intangible itch hiding between the firings of our frontal lobes. For as long as we have had formalized arts, we have had competition around them. As previously discussed, Greek drama was directly built around festival competition, with rich Athenians riding dramatic geniuses like thoroughbreds into winner's circles. Poetry competitions, formal and informal, are at least as old as the impulse to write poetry down, from aristocratic and bureaucratic quill-measuring in Chinese and Japanese courts to the Floral Games, a sort of proto-Battle of the Bands for medieval French and Catalan troubadours. There were even artistic competitions in the

Olympics from 1912 to 1948 (breakdancing also made an appearance at the Paris 2024 games, although it was immediately dropped), ultimately cancelled only because technically every artist was a professional, violating the spirit of amateurism that was then important.

These days, direct, head-to-head competition is generally frowned upon once an artist has reached a certain level of import or has something to say about Drake, but implied, indirect competition remains at the root of nearly all of our artistic, literary, and performing prizes. There have been scattered individual purses, and titles like poet laureate once had more of a congratulatory angle, but our modern proclivity for this stuff can trace its roots to the French Academy pre- and post-revolution, most specifically in the Montyon Prizes. Founded by Antoine Jean Baptiste Robert Auget, Baron de Montyon, they were – much like their spiritual successor, the Nobel Prize – related not specifically to art but to advancing the cause of humanity in general, literature being one of four noble causes to which Montyon willed twelve thousand francs (the others were for making an industrial process less unhealthy; making a technical improvement to a mechanical process; and, to give you some insight into the base world view of self-proclaimed philanthropists, the 'prix de vertu,' awarded specifically to a 'poor Frenchman' who had completed the year's most courageous act – at least among the poors).

The type and variety of prizes and awards for artistic achievement have expanded somewhat gratuitously, ranging from the classic glitzy industry prizes of the EGOT (or whatever your particular country's version of those letters are) to a smattering of less publicly known but usually more cash-focused prizes, awarding everything from books translated into or from specific languages, to emerging dancers at notable ballet companies, to the more classic 'it would be uncouth to say "best," but if this prize goes the way we're hoping, you will de facto come to understand it as "best" book/album/painting/whatever of the year.

Without taking anything away from anyone who has ever won anything, you probably need only a passing understanding of even just post-Hollywood-awards-show chatter to get the idea that, as far as actually judging the artistic merits of what they're purporting to judge, awards are universally useless. This isn't really the fault of anyone who funds or judges or submits to them or takes them seriously (well, maybe a little bit of the latter) so much as an Inherent Contradiction of Judging Art: actors and sculptors and writers don't have established rule books or tightly controlled playing fields, let alone counting stats and advanced analytics. These judgments are wildly subjective interpretations of pieces and performances that are trying to give brief instantiation to the ineffable, and as such will be inextricably linked to prevailing aesthetic, moral, political, social, and gut judgments mildly inexplicable to the people making the decisions themselves, and could change as soon as the jury opens the deliberation room door. No, in the modern context, the purpose of awards is marketing: primarily for the generosity and wisdom of whoever the title sponsor and awarding body are, and then incidentally, but often quite life-changingly, for whoever takes home the prize.

A good general rule is that if no one outside your field or geographic area (depending on the exact criteria) has heard of whatever the award is, it is worth roughly whatever the cheque attached to it says. The household-name awards may come with bigger cheques (although none of those EGOT-level prizes have any cash attached to them, mostly because if you're in that conversation the amount of money they could realistically attach to them is no longer very meaningful) but also much, much more attention – and, if you have a product, sales, both immediately and for a certain portion of the future. It's relatively rare for these things to go to someone who doesn't have some level of stature or experience, but they can absolutely be the difference between muddling along in the in-between and being able to keep doing it for life: in 2017, for instance, Canadian poet and novelist Michael Redhill celebrated the $100,000 Giller Prize by posting the bank receipt he got for depositing the cheque, which showed his balance at a cool $100,411.

Prizes of all stripes, even the rich and celebrated ones, are just the most distilled example of the lottery-esque logic of arts in the marketplace. Literally just one person is plucked out of a host of worthy options, getting all the rewards while the others sate themselves on the niceties of being nominated/published/represented, having a steady job, etc. The awards do offer one little bonus that the regular market does not, though: thanks to their desperately maintained sense of prestige and legitimacy, and the natural conservatism that comes from money and from group decisions, and the undeserved but obvious attention they garner, they're very useful for sussing out when certain modes of creation and expression have passed over from the realm of Something Else into the realm of Art. Which brings me to ContraPoints.

———

Natalie Wynn, who creates YouTube videos on the channel ContraPoints, is, at the time of writing, the only YouTube-based creator to have ever been awarded a Peabody. Created in 1940 as the broadcast equivalent of the Pulitzers (at the time, 'broadcast' meant radio but quickly expanded to include television), the Peabodys are essentially Olympic medals for prestige television, recognizing achievements in journalism and documentary but also giving space and lifetime achievement awards to fictional shows and the people who make them. Stephen Colbert has a few, and so do shows like *The Sopranos, Atlanta, Twin Peaks, The Simpsons, Mad Men* – anything that has earned a critical reputation for pushing the boundaries of television. In 2022, the award saw fit to push its own boundaries and created the 'Immersive and Interactive' category, kind of a catch-all for online-y/digital-y things that didn't have a natural home elsewhere. So far it's mostly amounted to some video games, a *New Yorker* VR experience, and ContraPoints.

In fairness to the Peabodys, Wynn's ContraPoints project is not easy to classify, at least not if you are trying to analyze the channel from the ground up. Top down, it's a YouTube channel, specifically in the lineage of the straight-to-camera vlog, wherein a person essentially just points the camera at themselves and talks. PewDiePie, whose channel was once number one on YouTube, is a vlogger, as were the stars of most of the platform-specific breakout channels – one of the earliest viral vlog hits, the gradually revealed mystery story *lonelygirl15*, figured out how to futz with the format by telling a fictional story in 2006 – although the vast difference between yelling shit at video games and what Wynn is up to suggests how limited the term 'vlogger' is. Another mostly digitally native way of talking about what she does would be to say she's a video essayist, someone who makes long-form videos that examine aspects of culture or art or politics, sort of the YouTube version of the think piece: somewhat academic in approach but decidedly more broad and inviting in both tone and subject, and actively plugged into the discourse as opposed to rescuing subjects from obscurity.

These are, if I can be a little grandiose, as close to a fully formed-by-the-platform art form as YouTube has. Whereas a lot of the most popular YouTube videos and channels are essentially pre-existing forms distilled through millennial/ Gen Z/Gen A cultural understandings (talk shows, sketch comedy, prank shows, game shows, explainer shows, documentaries), these are a type of thing that didn't properly exist before the wild democratization of film equipment and distribution. Essay films certainly existed, and in some sense that same transliteration is going on here, but everything from the subject matter to the purpose has been massively altered by immediacy. Wynn offers everything from four-hour-plus epic dissections of amusement parks and their place in the collective psyche to deep dives into crypto scams via parodies of hustle bro culture to slightly less formally chaotic but still impressively broad considerations of film, philosophy, influencer culture, YouTube creator drama, and everything else.

Wynn began ContraPoints as an explicitly political project, providing alternative interpretations and understandings of some of the virulently right-wing information that was growing on YouTube in the wake of Gamergate and the rise of Trump, informed by her own gender transition. Early videos were something between leftist explainers of the forces that gave us fascist alt-right mobs, incels, and Jordan Peterson, and gentle and often highly personal off-ramps for anyone falling down those particular rabbit holes. Even these early videos veered away from simple categorization: besides being willing to thoroughly analyze 4chan and Reddit threads as closely as philosophy texts (Wynn was pursuing a PhD in the subject before abandoning academia), she was pushing the boundaries of the talking-head video, employing elaborate costumes and sets, staging one-act plays and Socratic dialogues with characters, all played by Wynn, modelled after online tropes. She also started expanding her area of consideration to topics ripped from Twitter feeds (cancelling, and J. K. Rowling's whole thing) and more generally bubbling up through the human condition (envy, shame, men).

Now, maybe this isn't quite art, yet. A lot of Wynn's contemporaries might be doing something closer to the YouTube equivalent of a magazine deep dive or a well-researched op-ed. Even if we are willing to say Wynn transcends that form, maybe her work is fundamentally too something – factual? political? rhetorical? static? didactic? – to quite qualify as art. Even my use of the Peabodys was kind of a cheat here: although half of the awards' attention is devoted to documentaries and fictional TV shows, the other half is to self-admitted journalistic endeavours. Maybe it's just that.

But at the very least, I think we are witnessing the emergence of, if not an entirely new art form, at least a profoundly unique style of film, one that could become some people's most consistent and cherished engagement with it. And the mix of incentives pushing this down the birth canal are worth examining.

———

In many ways, YouTube is just the most shining example of the promise that digital distribution was supposed to bring to a class that didn't really have an accepted name but that we've now insisted upon calling 'creators.' (And it's worth taking a beat here to remind ourselves that promises are about intent, not execution.) A world where distribution was as easy as pushing a button was going to usher in the end of gatekeepers and middlemen; allow people making the things to interact directly with the people who wanted them; and create a kind of meritocratic free-for-all where the visionaries and geniuses could rise, unfettered by the purse-clutching suits that were the accepted enemies of good art.

This was always a little bit bullshit, but like most techy bullshit it did at least bring to light some of the serious drawbacks of what it was trying to replace, which can make something seem like the only true path forward. Having to convince an ever-expanding cast of increasingly unrelated middle managers that what you're doing is worthy of being seen is not a system that is going to make expression, innovation, or idiosyncrasy all that easy, and those are all pretty bedrock ideas in the pursuit of interesting art. That system left a considerable body count of dreams and dreamers in its wake, giving grifters, scammers, or even just the terminally clueless plenty of opportunity to muck things up at the cost of the artist. However much the industry was unfairly clawing away from artists, though, people were getting something from it: not having to also be skilled self-promoters, for instance. Or the maintenance of a network of fellow professionals supported by the dribs and drabs of work that sloughed off the main body, a network you could call on and even slink into between your own bursts of creation.

On the positive side of the ledger, there's also a lot of tinder in this new model for an inferno of attempts to do things. In the case of YouTube, the barrier to entry is essentially just a smartphone, although a reliable Wi-Fi connection is also important. Almost everyone who is making a serious go of these things has upgraded their set-up considerably, but we are still in an era where some of the most prominent voices did not have anything resembling training – or even much exposure to the types of things they were trying to create, because examples didn't really exist yet. True, genres like blues or punk didn't require much more than a guitar, but they also did not come with any inherent expectation of audience, and especially not an audience of complete strangers; the idea that you could go from flicking on your camera as you walk out of the Apple Store to addressing the world is enough to spark the creative fires of plenty of people who don't have the patience for a G chord.

Opening the doors to an infinite number of monkeys is relatively small potatoes, though, compared to what it has meant for finding an audience. The vast majority of creators will not find much of an audience, certainly not enough of one to be handsomely or even healthily recompensed. But this economy in all its platforms has opened up alleys and avenues that hadn't previously existed; it doesn't seem to have increased the overall pool of money, nor broken up the basic structure whereby a small number of people get an outsized share of rewards, nor done much to correct the fact that many of those people have nothing whatsoever to do with the actual creation of art. BUT! To the degree that it does put some money in the hands of the people making things, it has broken a handful of massive pyramids into dozens of smaller ones. So let us take our victories where we can.

In the case of ContraPoints, Wynn has an audience of about 1.8 million subscribers on YouTube. Most of her videos end up with view counts double or triple that, which would matter if she did things like sponsorships or allowed YouTube ads, but she has instead opted to get all of her financial support from Patreon, the money-collecting platform that 'gives you a direct line of access to your fan community.' Those are impressive viewing numbers, although a blip in the sorts of stats that YouTube deals in: she has vastly outperformed the almost 97 percent of channels that don't manage a thousand subscribers, but is not even close to entering the top ten thousand worldwide. YouTube claims about 2.5 billion active users; even if we limit ourselves to North America, Wynn's existing audience would amount to about two-thirds of a percent of her theoretically possible audience. Her lot doesn't improve much if we turn to Patreon: of ContraPoints' 1.8 million YouTube subscribers, only 26,840 have seen fit to pay her for what she's producing. Patreon is a bit secretive about the exact amounts its creators make, but even if we just assume Wynn's subscribers are all using the lowest possible tier of paid subscription, two entire U.S. dollars per month, that would put her current annual income somewhere in the range of 600,000 USD (Patreon takes between 5 and 12 percent). I am not sure by what mechanism a trans woman doing single-hander Socratic dialogues about the nature of envy would have found that sort of payday pre-2016, though I do know some people who broadly fit that description but took more traditional routes and would be quite ecstatic to have made two weeks' worth of her income for the year (especially if it was every year).

We cannot escape this without caveats. The first being that this is pretty much the absolute peak: Wynn is one of the top five video creators on Patreon in terms of paid subscribers, and one of the top twenty in the world in any category. And the fall-off is steep: the fiftieth-place project has about half as many subscribers, and fewer than 900 Patreon users, out of more than 250,000, have more than one hundred paid subscribers. Patreon estimates that its average active creator makes about $315 a month on average, which accounts for about 41 percent of their income from creative or creative-related business projects. So the vast majority of creators on Patreon have some kind of other work as well, especially if the top creators are included in that calculation of average. (Half of Patreon's employees make more than $150,000 a year; we don't know how many of them create on the platform.)

YouTube is less explicitly about supporting creators, which introduces its own set of challenges. Like any social platform, it is prone to making changes to how things are discovered, or downplaying certain expressions or language, or just generally behaving like a black box that can dictate your visibility and thus viability on a platform that rewards attention. It has ad structures and subscription models that are tangentially about rewarding people who make things, though the company has enough money that even a small fraction of it is massive. In early 2024, YouTube claimed it had given creators more than 70 billion USD over the previous three years. This would have been earned at an average rate of between 0.2 and 1.8 cents per view, which should give you some sense of the Lovecraftian terror of how much time the world is spending on YouTube; things get more abyssal when you consider that less than 9 percent of YouTube accounts make even $50 a month from the platform.

The overwhelming scale of it all means that a significant number of people are making something off it, but it doesn't give you better odds of making money off art in the grand scheme. Especially considering that so much of what you're competing against isn't even crafted specifically for the platform, nor does the vast majority of the platform have any intention of making art. Which speaks to one of the underlying problems of the online platform model in general: as much as it makes it possible for any random creator to reach everyone, it also makes it much easier for that potential audience to consume everything. At least when there were gatekeepers, you knew who you had to impress. In an age of algorithmic mass audience, the problem is not just making something interesting, or even really standing out from the crowd, it's figuring out how to get yourself in front of a sufficient number of eyes in the first place. People have done it and continue to do it, some more cravenly than others, but at the scope we are talking about here, I'm not sure there's much more than random chance at play: even if we concede that everyone who gains a following has done something to deserve it, somewhere in that 91 percent of $50-or-lessers are thoughtful, interesting, boundary-pushing creators who just never got the right break.

Which is maybe how it's always been. But if these revolutionary platforms are not much more than a subtle tweak to the model of paying artists, they are at least creating space for new kinds of things to flourish. It is hard to be terribly optimistic about which kinds of things, to be honest. For every ContraPoints, there are thousands of projects that seem absolutely overwhelmed by the immediacy of the audience, flattening themselves into cheap flattery of their viewers, and shamelessly aiming to be relatable or identifiable or dopamine-fuelling enough to justify the subscription price. If this sounds familiar, remember that similar complaints were levelled against theatre in Rome, when the audience could take money back from the performers if they didn't like the show.

Maybe it's just my turn in the cycle of a perpetual complaint, but I find it hard to take in some of the forms most at home on these direct-audience platforms and not think art has been thoroughly eviscerated by money, clawed apart by the invisible hand. Keeping closest to what I do, the most uniquely endemic form of writing on Patreon is a genre of fiction known as LitRPG, or sometimes Progression Fantasy. (Patreon is a vast endeavour, but while it features plenty of writers, it's not even the primary creator platform used by writers, which might be Wattpad or maybe Substack, depending on your style of writing. But because Patreon is explicitly for getting paid for creating, it's a good barometer for types of writing that prioritize that aspect.) Equal parts video game recap and weaponized power fantasy – 'power fantasy' is often used with a negative connotation, but these books are praised as *the* power fantasies by their paying fans – these stories are essentially first-person accounts of what it might be like to be the main character in an RPG video game. They are crafted to appeal to the sort of person who wants to spend any time they're not actually playing RPG video games experiencing someone else do it, but who draws the line at watching any of the voluminous number of YouTube channels that offer that (those channels present people actually playing games; LitRPG is about what it would be like to be a character in a made-up version of those games). Owing to their intimate connection with publication on Patreon, where the monthly subscription format and subsequent audience expectation encourage frequent and consistent publishing, they are clockwork creations, with instalments coming out in some cases daily, and sagas stretching to one thousand chapters and counting.

As someone who has never been fully immune to the specialist-boy undercurrent in a lot of popular fantasy stories, I am still fully baffled by the appeal of this particular genre. The stories are, to a sentence, artless. They amount to the stenography of an imagined world, like hearing someone emotionlessly recount their Tetris dreams. They need to exist on a platform without gatekeepers, because it is hard to imagine that anyone who has sufficiently devoted themselves to reading to make it a job would ever believe someone would pay to read this. Writers of this genre currently occupy four of the top five spots in the Writing category of Patreon; Zogarth, the writer of the *Primal Hunter* series, who helpfully openly discloses his earnings, is number three, with over eight thousand subscribers contributing $63,000 a month. In the three years since he began writing *Primal Hunter*, he has claimed to have earned more than seven figures from selling collections of the nine-hundred-plus-chapter story on Amazon. This makes him rather easily one of the most financially successful writers of fiction of his generation; assuming she got a standard 10 percent royalty, Sally Rooney – who I think it's fair to say occupies a slightly more significant place in the public consciousness – would have made about $1.3 million in the first three years of her career (which, to be fair, only included two, much shorter, books).

The only thing that prevents me from curling up into a ball after viewing those numbers is wondering what this will spawn. One of the constants of the evolution of art is that people end up where the money is; it was only about sixty years ago that fantasy and science fiction more broadly would have been met with a similar sort of revulsion as the gut-level heave I feel reading sentences like 'Walking down the stairs to his car, he had an intuition that the day was going to be interesting. He didn't know why as everything was as usual so far, but he couldn't entirely dispel the feeling.' (To be clear, that is within the first two hundred words of *The Primal Hunter*, the part that is meant to get you to keep reading it.) But someone out there is willing to pay for it, enough someones to make it a consistently paying job with a reach that far exceeds its place in the polished literary consciousness.

Sci-fi pulp magazines like *Amazing Stories*, which had its heyday from the 1930s to the 1960s, were considered notoriously cheap: Hugo Gernsback, the editor who would give the now-prestigious Hugo Awards their name, was nicknamed 'The Rat' by some of his more famous authors and paid rates of about a quarter of a cent per word, rolling up to a whole penny and a half if you were a recognizable name. Adjusted for inflation, this amounts to about five to twenty-seven cents per word. Not livable rates, but still miles better than what contemporary authors might make: the highest-paying equivalent now, *Analog Science Fiction and Fact*, tops out at eight cents a word. At times there were dozens of outlets accepting stories at those rates; there are plenty of places to submit work now, but few that will guarantee you anything other than the chance to be published, and maybe edited, too.

This was lucrative enough to bring people to the table, and with a ravenous fan base that read sci-fi and fantasy widely and deeply, all of these writers had to experiment with the language they were using, the sort of stories they were telling, and precisely how they were told. If you get enough of that – not quite an infinite amount – things will be created that resonate. Even the basest commercialism can result in works that alter our perception of the world and don't merely let us escape into flattering fantasy. Science fiction and fantasy have not just been entirely legitimated, they have produced some of the most popular and resonant works of art of the twenty-first century. Why shouldn't a similar process happen to LitRPG, or any other online art form that can draw an audience?

Just as the video games that inspire LitRPG continue to expand their complexity of storytelling and integration of the medium's mechanics, why wouldn't someone, perhaps confident that they can clear an annual salary in a month just by writing down their fantasies, eventually produce Shakespeare? Or, anyway, a first-person video game RPG narrative that says something piercingly unique about the human condition? Every variation on a theme will produce something new, some evolution that may prove advantageous in the field of what we consider literary art. The surest way to get lots of variations is to make people think that doing this work could pay their rent.

It would be a mistake to assume that the creators who use these platforms are being paid solely for their output. They are also being paid, sometimes rather explicitly, for themselves or, anyway for a level of direct access to their process and personal life that would once have been nearly unimaginable, at least if we limit ourselves to the last few hundred years. Royal and aristocratic patrons certainly had a pretty unfettered access to their artists, and often considered the personal relationship to be part of what they were paying the artist for. But nothing like this has ever existed on a mass scale: earning, or even attempting to earn, your living off a platform comes with an expectation of interactivity with a large group of people. That requires a temperament as rare as any that can produce resonating art.

At a minimum, this means submitting your work to the instant reaction and potentially wavering financial support of your audience, many of whom, though they describe themselves as fans, are more brutally critical than any outside observer or even nominally impartial professional critic would ever be. In the age of social media, every level and kind of artist goes through some version of this, but people directly paid via online platforms don't have the luxury of being able to float above this sort of interaction. It also means a level of active engagement – responding to comments and soliciting feedback or suggestions – that can rival the actual work in terms of time spent. Some creators maintain entirely separate platforms where their customers can discuss their work and suggest or vote on other topics or creative choices for future projects. Discords are popular these days, but YouTube recently announced the creation of a 'Community' feature that will let subscribers directly post their reactions to and remixes of their favourite creators' work. Whatever your intentions or goals, living on these platforms means submitting to the dictates of branding and accessibility that define them. Some people can create a perpetually sustaining fandom that doesn't require direct maintenance, but vanishingly few can get to that point without actively pursuing this mixture of customer service and self-promotion for years, usually for next to no money. Not even the highest earners, after all, emerged onto these platforms fully formed with a ready audience of thousands.

If the pessimistic view of this added layer of responsibility focuses on the extra burden on artists and the potential creative pitfalls of being too responsive to audience sensibility, the optimistic view calls us back to the practicalities, if not necessarily the loftier ideals, of earlier DIY movements. Getting out from behind the curtain to sell yourself and whatever you're making to the person who came out to your show is a model consistently celebrated to this day. That's more a case of fighting back against the intermediary corporate forces controlling our world than helping them stoke their engagement numbers. Still, both require a similar mindset and set of skills, none of which are explicitly related to making art.

———————

The modern conception of DIY was created in 1980s punk scenes, with notables like Fugazi avoiding record labels, playing cheap shows – they had a five-dollar-show rule for many years – outside traditional venues, and encouraging people to create networks devoted to DIY ethics in every city they toured. This has more or less persisted at a low buzz in major cities across North America for a few decades since, although like most things not fanatically devoted to making money, it hasn't been entirely helped by the internet era. For a time, though, it looked like the wild networks the internet allowed for might be ideal for something like a nationally unified DIY scene. Among the first bands to take a swing was Bomb the Music Industry!, who were kind enough to wear their allegiance to alternative models on the spray-painted T-shirts they sold as merch.

Begun in the suburbs of New York with a PowerBook recording by Jeff Rosenstock, Bomb the Music Industry! evolved into a collective band and the world's first entirely by-donation record label, Quote Unquote Records, both animated by Rosenstock's endless energy. Rosenstock embraced both the disembodied disconnection of digital possibilities and the primal necessity of face-to-face interactions. All the band's music was released free online, though you could donate whatever you wanted for it. You could not purchase any kind of physical copy, but if you brought a blank CD to their show, they would burn their albums onto it for you. This was the only way to get merch, as well: bring a shirt and they'd stencil on their name in spray paint. This intimate interaction – in which familiar artifacts of commerce become another act of creation on the part of the artist, providing a moment together talking and waiting for the thing to be made – is why the band has become an almost folkloric legend among a select group. That and the fact they confined themselves to cheap, all-ages shows anywhere that would let them plug in an amp.

Blessed though his community spirit is, Rosenstock's model requires the devotion of time and energy to activities that have more to do with the promotion of art than its creation. The admirable absence of economic drive does not make the process easier. Every artist of sufficient public attention knows how to toot their own horn, but there's a difference between cultivating a variety of skills and making all of them a prerequisite for making something other people might experience. Better to do that in the service of community than the service of shareholders, but art needs space for introverts, too. However noble the rejection of money as motivation, it's money that can buy you a publicist. Still, it's hard to argue with any concept of putting your art out there in a way that earns you the eternal goodwill of a devoted audience, even if that audience is smaller than the one you could have paid more for.

I have trouble picturing a world where this imperative to allow access to the artist, not just the art, weakens. For starters, the desire to know more about, interact with, understand on some personal level the people who create the art we like is as old as signing a name to that art. Biography, criticism, gossip, and odd devotion are basic consequences of being an artist. Selling those things is not quite as old, but is still pretty established, and recent methods have made them easier and more immediate. Now that those doors are open, they begin to look like the natural path. We hear laments about the level of access and intimacy demanded of some artists, but those are from people who have already navigated the new system. You can always pull back once you've reached a certain threshold, but that doesn't change the gauntlet people have to run to get there. The sheer amount of art – let alone pure distraction – that exists in this world, old and new, demands that you find some way to flag people's attention; creating a community around yourself, for fun or profit, is good marketing and a sign that your art might mean something to people. I'm not much for the idea that something like an artificial intelligence will come along and replace artists in any meaningful way, but playing up your real human opinions and experiences does cut through some of the ways vast corporate behemoths try to drag the artists out of art. And hey: those same companies will maybe give you some money and support if you've already done the work of proving there's an audience for you.

There's always more an artist should be willing to do, and you do want to be an artist, don't you?

Whatever other potential schemes emerge for giving artists some portion of the money they create, the prevailing trend is demanding extraneous labour and reverse-siphoning the vast majority of money to people removed from anything resembling creative work. And this will likely reinforce what has always been true: that the best and most reliable way to make a living at the arts is to come from money. There is no better source of non-artistic income than one that places no extra demands on your time or productive energy, requires no lengthy explanation of your vision (depending on the family, I suppose), comes with built-in access to people well-off enough to buy whatever you end up selling, promises a steady drip through early stages of exploration and integration, and then potentially floods you with cash mid-career.

A cursory knowledge of more than one or two artists who have ever lived will tell you that the independently wealthy have a vastly easier go of it in the arts (and life). One of the most exhaustively granular studies on the matter comes from Karol Jan Borowiecki, an economist at the University of Southern Denmark. His expansive 2019 study, *The Origins of Creativity: The Case of the Arts in the United States Since 1850*, combed through census data in the United States to offer some definitive truths about what life has been like for artists. The connection between coming from money and making a life as an artist is a virtual model of linear progression: Borowiecki estimates that, from 1850 until his data runs dry in 2017, for every $10,000 more your family made per year, you were 2 percent likelier to end up in some sort of creative field. Though the real numbers are still pretty small, the odds stack up perfectly with the cash: a person whose family wealth is ten times yours is ten times more likely to have an artistic career, however much that career actually pays. Translate that to work ethic or lucky happenstance or freewheeling lack of concern for consequence or whatever your particular socio-economic theory of the world demands, but it's still a lot more grindstones and good coin flips necessary the further down you go. (And again, this is not a projection: these are the results over almost 170 years.)

I don't know of any Danish studies on the matter, but family money certainly feels like the most sensitive of subjects as far as money in the arts is concerned. There is often considerable cultural capital tied up in the artist who struggled and strived to get where they are, probably because it's so relatively rare. I mean, starting from the bottom is the default official biography of at least three or four genres of music (rap, punk, blues, country, although maybe not so much anymore), and the shortest route to authenticity in any art form. So no wonder the idea that your life before art was cozy and quaint, that it came with every bit of encouragement or training or equipment or just time and space, would be something most people would want to downplay or elide. Also doesn't hurt that artists are supposed to be about ideas and passions and their calling; rich people love to talk about anything other than money. There's no particular justification for growing up with money; but however dirty, crushing, or suspect a side gig might be, you earned that money. Rich parents are a lottery you don't even have to sully yourself to play.

To be clear, nothing about family money tarnishes whatever art is produced; the idea of the romantic struggle is a coping mechanism as much as anything, and the weight of something truly expressed hits the same no matter how much it cost. There's more than a little self-justification in that sentiment, I'm sure: I don't come from aristocrats or even business owners, but I married someone whose judge dad paid for her private school, and access to her family has improved my chances of sustaining a creative career by at least ten times (even more so given that she has a good enough job that I don't have to maximize my earning potential to

keep us in a position to eat at farmers markets and vacation
to other cities) (thank you, baby, I love you for reasons well
beyond that). I feel appropriately guilty about that, I assure
you, enough to point out that even with the help I have had,
I am at best about the average for people who make a go of
creative careers. So save your snide comments about my
unearned subsidy for mediocrity for, say, the photographer
whose parents own a chain of successful car washes, or the
Hollywood nepo babies.

But more to the point, I do not want to live in a world
that provides any fewer opportunities for artists, rich or otherwise. But I do think that art is diminished when the only real
opportunities are for people who are essentially retirees
pursuing a hobby. Acknowledging family money, and maybe
even trying to make that level of forthrightness something
to aspire to – maybe even as celebrated as pulling-yourself-
out-of-dirt-poordom – strikes me as a deceptively important
step in the evolution of art, a way to shake the foundations
of a crucial but restricted aspect of being a relatively complete
human being. (I mean, I guess we could also just give every-
body a Universal Basic Income and see what happens, though
I'm not sure which is less realistic at this point.)

––––––––––

One of the main criteria by which we celebrate art is its sense
of honesty about the world. The nebulousness of both 'art'
and 'honesty' as terms should give you some sense of how
much we're in the realm of gut feeling here, but that is the
root of the connection, I think. Perhaps it is something as
simple as recognizing a bit of the world the same way a piece
of art does: getting the same rush of overwhelming beauty

from a chaotically bright forest scene or seeing ourselves in the sweetly desperate fumbling of a person talking to someone they very much want to kiss. Sometimes it is admiring a spikier or more bitter honesty, appreciating that someone is able to peel back the gauze of sentiment and purposeful ignorance of something we've experienced and let the whiff of a raw wound drift through the air. Sometimes it is just capturing a sentiment or expression with such sparkling clarity that we, the audience, are left grasping at words to make our feelings concrete and settle on 'that's true' for lack of any better feeling to pin it on. Part of the point of art has always been to show us the world as it really feels to us, which is about as close as we are able to get to knowing how it is, and who we are in it.

At the risk of hanging one more unreasonable demand around the neck of artists, I don't think the force that gives the label of 'artist' meaning should be left out of that search for a true thing. Perhaps my most enduringly pessimistic view is that we'll never really be free of the struggle and status and competition and constriction that money embodies, but you certainly can't free yourself of a thing until you fully embrace what it has done to you.

Nothing comes for free, not even making art.

Conclusion: Sing It Yourself

When I began this project, I assumed that the reason money was so often overlooked in the discussion of the arts boiled down to the miasmic shame that envelops the subject in our culture in general. Whether you have too much of it or too little – there doesn't really seem to be a right amount – there is a pervasive hint in our culture that you should shut up about it, downplay it, maybe outright lie about it, but anyway, certainly not open up your soul or your wallet and lay bare what exactly it means to you. Doubly so when that would get in the way of the nobler aspirations of the creative, artistic spirit.

I might run on a higher-octane shame than average, but there's been almost no point of the process of writing this book that hasn't sent me on a spiral into some level of shame. I mean, the historical bits, I guess, are distant enough to not cause any crying in the shower, but any amount of self-reflection or even contemporary consideration is a peat bog of potential horrors. Is my complete inability to support myself through standard capitalist means definitive proof of my unworthiness as an artist? Does the fact I'm able to rely on a certain level of unearned material comfort mean I am essentially stealing the wind from the sails of a smarter, sharper, obviously better writer who wasn't able to marry into a reliable savings account? Does the fact I've knowingly accepted lower advances than friends and compatriots reveal that I am a shit negotiator who will never have the skills to survive in a vast, uncaring industry that is way better at this than me? If I did more social media, would I have a better or more lucrative job? Did I fuck up by not pursuing enough advanced degrees to get a teaching job? I am tempted to say that there is no end to the rabbit hole, but I don't think rabbit holes are typically lined with barbed spikes tipped with a neurotoxin designed to make you apologize to all your loved ones for failing them while you choke to death. Economists, at least, don't have to ask themselves such questions (although I wonder how often they do economic analyses of how much economists make).

If I encountered anything to rival this socio-economic self-loathing, it has to have been the perpetual bleakness of the economic outlook for making virtually any form of art. I realize this is not exactly headline news – it's something between a cliché and an autonomic system reaction to tell any youth foolish enough to say they want to devote themselves to the arts that it's real tough out there, you should have a backup plan, et cetera and so forth. But I think we tend to think of it only in the most grandiose terms: like, sure, if your dream is to become a movie star – or, I guess, in modern terms, MrBeast – that's gonna be a tough road. I don't think it takes very long on anyone's journey – well, anyone's journey that doesn't involve the Disney Channel, stage parents, and teenaged success – to figure this out; I have been keenly aware that selling out was going to be less a case of laptop-shaped pools and more a case of being able to afford rent after I no longer had access to any sort of scholarship or student loan.

But the rampant existence of art schools and improv classes and manuscript workshops and all that other stuff also, I think, suggests there is a baseline belief that making some kind of living is within your grasp. And, absolutely, some kind is: probably some kind wherein your creative pursuits are pieced together in between entirely other ways to pay the bills. If you are lucky, these other pursuits will be close enough to what you do that they'll be considered adjunct or at least complementary; if you were born lucky, it will come in the form of some member of your family, dead or alive, subsidizing your pursuits. Likely you'll need some combination of both. It's only if you are absurdly fortunate that you will make a reasonable living at this, devoting the bulk of your time and identity to just making stuff while still maintaining something like the average standard of living for your particular neck of the woods. And this is not some anomaly or recent downturn; if anything, things have probably gotten better, owing to the improvement of the standard of living and average leisure time since industrialization. (Or, anyway, gotten better and are now on a bit of a downward trend again, although still a ways above the historical mean.)

Even if that whole scenario is common knowledge, it is one thing to 'know' it somewhere in the vague distances of the back of your brain, and another to force it into your frontal lobe for any length of time, to really confront it, sit with it, and then stand up and start working again. The romantic in me would like to call that a leap of faith, the cynic an act of ego, but it's probably something more like the fuzzy ignorance that makes so much of life possible, if not necessarily worthwhile. (That's not to take anything away from faith or ego. It's just that starting a journey requires big speeches and fresh resolve, whereas continuing one really just requires you to not give up, which in my experience has to do with not giving a lot of space or time to the reasons to give up.) It is a lot easier to get things done when you're not constantly confronted by the cold realities of life. Not in a Pollyanna way, just in a more straight-ahead sense. Thinking about how your actions will serve the people who love you now has a little more practical utility than reminding yourself that no one, not even your blood descendants, if you have any, will remember your name two hundred years hence. (I mean, maybe they will! Because of this book! But, again, playing the odds here.)

The solution to this – the preferred method of inducing fuzzy ignorance – is supposed to be to love the process, the craft, the doing. Which, I mean, sure, do that. I'm sorry, I don't mean to be flip, but that advice is one of those clichés so brutally, unfortunately true that saying it will never mean a damn thing. It just has to sneak into your being while you're otherwise occupied, until one day you wake up and feel its dull ache in your bones and have to accept that this is just a horrible, huge part of what life is: a bunch of things figured out before you were born that you'll never be able to teach anyone.

I do kinda love the process enough of the time. (I definitely love having conversations with myself, which is enough of the process to matter.) But that's not a terribly meaningful hedge when I'm halfway through a life that has been specifically chosen and arranged around trying to make this a living. If I only intuited this before, two years of deep confrontation and historical research on the matter have effectively confirmed that the most realistic best-case scenario for My Life as a Writer is basically what I have at the moment, extended until my heart or artificial brain give out. Yes, I could suddenly develop a talent for fantasy romance mystery novels, or chubby, sad, self-consciously literary Canadians who post biannually could become the hot new TikTok trend. Barring that, this is what my career will be, at least from a basic financial standpoint: I will piece together some combination of publicly available funds, dwindling savings, the goodwill of my family, time off from whatever thing is actually paying my bills, and the greatly appreciated but inevitably inadequate cheque the person who agrees to distribute my work will send my way, swirl them about for two to five years, and end up with a book that will make just enough money for someone else that I will be allowed to do it again (and again, and again). I would be *proud* to call that the rest of my career, honestly; if we drop the 'best case,' the most realistic scenario is that I probably get between one and three more of these, at which point the potential energy of my career and actual energy of my body is so drained I just keep a small box of each book at the back of increasingly diminishing closets until my grandchildren throw them away. (I suppose they might turn them into blown insulation or use them for fuel, depending on how various climate scenarios play out.)

That doesn't seem like a romantic or even especially appealing life, laid out like that. And yet and yet. I know that I am going to take swings at those one to three, and more if I get them. I know that I am going to forgo family time and probably more lucrative career options (until both of those things start to dry up entirely) and less stressful hobbies and some part of my health for the prospect of doing this again (and again), probably past the point of people telling me to just stop. I may persist because of some baseline delusion that the next one will be the one that puts me into that tier of the reasonably comfortable, if not the universally revered, but I don't think there's a lot of that delusion left. I think I do this just because I have to. Because I do not know any better, or I have built a sufficient part of my understanding of who I am in the world around it, or because I would be haunted if I did not keep trying. At this point in my life, it seems like enough to just feel secure that I know some part of who I am; the whys never seem to settle down, anyway.

For artists who aren't me, I think the future will look a lot like the past. A profoundly small few will make comfortable livings at it; maybe this few will be a bit more spread around various art forms and styles and genres than it used to be, but some outsized portion of the money that finds its way to art will go to a small number of artists, and the rest of the artists will muddle through in between doing other things. If you have to bet on a group really taking it on the chin in the near future, it's this middle tier: as good side gigs dry up and resources coalesce into fewer hands, there won't be the space and time to rely on their relatively meagre artist's earnings to justify their output. This will have a significant impact on the quality and quantity of art produced, even if it's not immediately apparent to outsiders. The best-case scenario would be that, almost entirely divorced from the ability to make a living at it, people turn resolutely to making art for themselves and their circles, and we begin a long, slow process of rebuilding a system that values art for its sake, and artists for theirs; maybe this time we can eventually arrive at a system that supports a more widespread creative impulse a little more equitably, although I don't know how optimistic I can be, at this point.

———————

A theory I have – which may also be my theory of why art is important at all – is that it is, overwhelmingly, through art that I've found experiences that obliterate all sense or rationality, that erase the itch for further explanation or tangible sense, that just emerge into my being and understanding as fundamentally true: real and undeniable as the heat of the sun on your skin on a cloudless day, or the encompassing satisfaction of cold water on the back of your throat. I think I just have to pursue that, try to capture it, and any amount – well, not *any* amount, but I'm trying to leave a little poetry in the world – of failure or false starts or deprivation or delaying of satisfaction is worth it if I can just grab a piece of that ineffability and maybe slip into the understanding of someone else out there.

It has taken me however many months and pages to land on a truth that I heard a long time ago in a song, 'Everything Is Free.' The words were written by Gillian Welch, although I first heard them being sung by Amelia Meath of Sylvan Esso and Jenn Wasner of Wye Oak and Flock of Dimes. I heard them again from maybe a half-dozen other artists before I finally came across Welch's version, although I think the fact it's well on its way to becoming one of the twenty-first century's first real folk songs speaks to the real transcendent truth of it. (If I can quote another piece of art that pierces me with authentic feeling: 'If it's never been new and it never gets old, it's a folk song.') Welch originally recorded and released it in 2001, in response to Napster and the first wave of file-sharing; this basic response hasn't lost a lick of its poignancy, at least from where I sit, but it's the resoluteness in the very first verse, where Welch conveys a certain pissed-off weariness while also using the alchemy of art's self-reflection to turn an admission of defeat into a rallying cry. I can't quote the lyrics, as it turns out; somewhat ironically, it would cost me about $1,500 to get even half a verse into this manuscript – $1,250 of which would go to the music publishing company, whose main contribution, as far as I can tell, was emailing me the price for quoting the lyrics. Fittingly enough, though, the final line makes note of the fact that anyone who creates stuff is going to keep creating anyway, however much money they actually get for it. That's one of those priceless truths art can convey. (I strongly recommend you go listen to the song. Preferably not on Spotify.)

So, yes, the entirety of my reality – not just my day-to-day life, but even my basic understanding of what kind of life I want it to be, my entire concept of 'being an artist' – owes itself to a bunch of people with a lot more money and just enough taste to align with my taste and self-conception. All of the art that has shaped my life is a function of these same forces. All of us who hold art in any regard have to acknowledge some debt to a class of probably far richer and more powerful and not necessarily more generous people who use these awesome expressions of what it means to be alive to burnish their own prestige, or at least their bank accounts. We are made of the mud of this world, after all; there is still some grace in pulling off pieces and trying to shape them into something beautiful.

———

I have a lot of thoughts and arguments for why we should make it easier – materially, but also spiritually and psycho-logically – for people to make art. Perhaps the most founda-tional one is nothing more than that we have been given the gifts of reflection and expression from somewhere, whether an intentional spark or an accident of animal flesh, and insofar as it is the rarest and most precious thing we have yet been able to find in the universe, we need to nurture it at almost any cost. We need to give ourselves the time and space to let these gifts show us their full potential. What's the worst possible outcome of arranging society to give people the maximum chance to show off what's at the core of their being? That we use up all Earth's resources and render it an exhausted wasteland?

But this is a book of material realities. And the reality is that we will keep up this striving to create, to grasp at the ineffable and give that same tiny piece of it back to the world, regardless of how easy or accessible or even feasible it is. This has been figured out for some time now – though for a long, long time it was only the most privileged and secure among us who even had a shot at exploring these things to their fullest extent – although I do worry that the brutal logic of exploiting our most human tendencies is only getting more efficient and refined. That something seems unkillable doesn't strike me as a reason to starve it; I have no doubt that we would find a way to whistle in our own graveyards. But really, what is the point of all this if we're not digging up the bones to find out why we're built this way?

Works Referenced

Abbing, Hans. *Why Are Artists Poor? The Exceptional Economy of the Arts.* Amsterdam University Press, 2002.

Benjamin, Walter. 'The Work of Art in the Age of Mechanical Reproduction' (1935). In *Illuminations*, edited by Hannah Arendt, translated by Harry Zohn. Schocken Books, 1969.

Byrne, David. *How Music Works.* McSweeney's, 2012.

Cennini, Cennino. *A Treatise on Painting.* Translated by Mary P. Merrifield. 1844.

Crow, Sara. *Never Get Tired: The Bomb the Music Industry Story* (documentary). 2015.

Csapo, Eric. *Actors and Icons of the Ancient Theater.* Wiley Blackwell, 2014.

Danto, Arthur. 'The Artworld.' *Journal of Philosophy* 61, no. 19 (Oct. 15, 1964): 571–84.

Fuller, Michael Anthony. *The Road to East Slope: The Development of Su Shi's Poetic Voice.* Stanford University Press, 1990.

Garber, Marjorie. *Patronizing the Arts.* Princeton University Press, 2008.

Gattinger, Monica. *The Roots of Culture, the Power of Art: The First Sixty Years of the Canada Council for the Arts.* McGill-Queen's University Press, 2017.

Hale, Sheila. *Titian: His Life.* Harper, 2012.

Hewison, Robert. *Culture and Consensus: England, Art and Politics Since 1940.* Routledge, 1997.

Litt, Paul. *The Muses, the Masses and the Massey Commission.* University of Toronto Press, 1992.

Lloyd, Rosemary. *Charles Baudelaire.* Reaktion, 2008.

Massey, Vincent (chair). Royal Commission on National Development in the Arts, Letters and Sciences 1949–1951.

Roberts, Michael James. *Tell Tchaikovsky the News: Rock 'n' Roll, the Labor Question, and the Musicians' Union, 1942–1968.* Duke University Press, 2014.

Rubin, Patricia Lee. *Giorgio Vasari: Art and History.* Yale University Press, 1995.

Warnke, Martin. *The Court Artist: On the Ancestry of the Modern Artist.* Translated by David McLintock. Cambridge University Press, 1993.

Acknowledgements

It seems as though the natural place to start here is to thank the Canada Council for their generous support of the creation of this book; I hope I did not say anything about your process that prevents me for receiving more of it. On that note, I'd also like to thank Believeco, the Edmonton Public Library, the Edmonton Arts Council, and the Edmonton Federation of Community Leagues for unwittingly subsidizing the creation of this work through employment that was gainful, but not too gainful. Thanks to the numerous freelance gigs that helped, too; you know who you are.

To my wonderful and exceptionally patient editor Alana, who by all rights should make as much as a registered psychologist, but will have to content herself with meagre but heartfelt sentiments such as 'I absolutely could not have done this without your infinite good sense and artistic compassion.' To my copyeditor Peter Norman, who understands my writing well enough to save me from myself as much as is reasonably possible.

To the wonderful artists who were willing to sit down and speak frankly with me when this book had a very different form, thanks for your time and what honesty you offered. Thanks to Mike and Kiara for gracefully listening to me explain every twist and turn of the process, and still being willing to talk. Thank you to Julie for always giving me something to think about. Thank you to Raymond for lending me your brilliant visual sensibility, and for being a model of the intelligence, dedication and ceaseless creativity that it takes to make it as an artist, now and from when I was much more wilfully ignorant, too. Thank you to Ron Garth, who gave me my first job thinking about art and who put up with my unwillingness to consider the material realities of artistic production with much more aplomb than was reasonable.

Thank you to my parents and my partner's parents, whose support, material and otherwise, is essential to this work. Thank you to my children for the constant reminder of why all this stuff is important. And thanks most of all to my partner, Nicki. Barnett Newman's wife, Annalee, once said of the seventeen years she spent working while he devoted himself to virtually unrecompensed painting and critique, 'For me it was no career. It was just a job. A job to earn a living so I could free my husband.' I actually can't picture you ever saying, or for that matter thinking, anything like that, but your support definitely feels just as extensive and all-encompassing.

Thanks to everyone who values cultural capital more than actual capital.

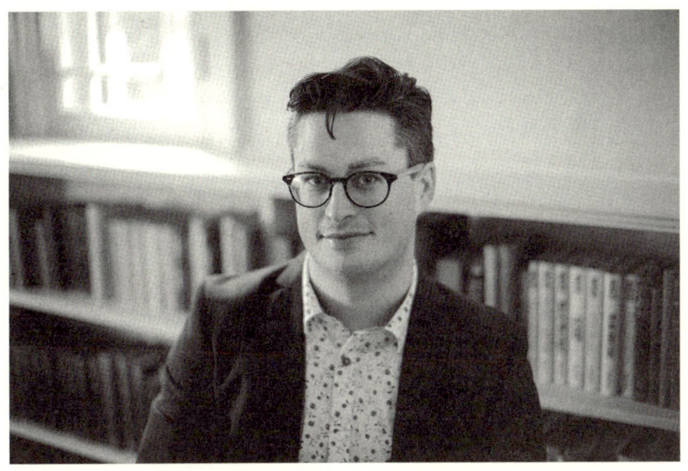

David Berry is a writer, editor, and critic. He spent the first two decades of his professional career profiling and critiquing the book, film, music, and theatre scenes for an Edmonton-based alt-weekly and then did the same nationally for the *National Post*. He has contributed essays, criticism, and features to the *Globe and Mail*, *The Walrus*, CBC, *Hazlitt*, and many other places, some of which still exist.

His first book, *On Nostalgia*, was published in summer 2020 by Coach House Books, just in time for everyone to suddenly become incredibly nostalgic for a time when they could actually see people and maybe even buy books in person. He lives in Edmonton with his partner and their two children, one of whom is both old enough to read and quite insistent on being referenced in this biography.

Typeset in Albertina and Helvetica Neue.

Printed at the Coach House on bpNichol Lane in Toronto, Ontario, on FSC-certified Sustana recycled paper, which was manufactured in Saint-Jérôme, Quebec. This book was printed with vegetable-based ink on a 1973 Heidelberg KORD offset litho press. Its pages were folded on a Baumfolder, gathered by hand, bound on a Sulby Auto-Minabinda, and trimmed on a Polar single-knife cutter.

Coach House Books is situated on occupied land that is the traditional territory of several Indigenous nations, including the Mississaugas of the Credit (an Anishnabek people), the Haudenosaunee Confederacy, and the Wendat and Petun nations, and is now home to many First Nations, Inuit, and Métis people. This land is covered by the Dish With One Spoon Covenant, an agreement between different First Nations communities to share resources peacefully and equitably, and by the Two-Row Wampum, a covenant of mutual respect and non-interference between early settlers and the Haudenosaunee. The land is also subject to Treaty 13, sometimes called the Toronto Purchase, signed between the settler colonists and the Mississaugas of the Credit.

As a settler organization, we acknowledge that we have violated these treaties and agreements. We acknowledge the grievous and ongoing harm of colonialism, and we strive to work toward a future of justice and reconciliation.

Edited by Alana Wilcox
Cover design by Raymond Biesinger
Interior design by Crystal Sikma
Author photo by Jessica Fern Facette

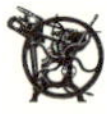

Coach House Books
80 bpNichol Lane
Toronto ON M5S 3J4
Canada
mail@chbooks.com
www.chbooks.com